Battle of Britain Aircraft

All plans mentioned in this book are available from ASP Plans Services, Argus House, Boundary Way, Hemel Hempstead, HP2 7ST. A catalogue is available on request, price £2.00 + 35p postage & packing.

Battle of Britain Aircraft

ARGUS
BOOKS

Argus Books
Argus House
Boundary Way
Hemel Hempstead
Hertfordshire HP2 7ST
England

First published by *Scale Models* Magazine 1982
This revised edition published by Argus Books 1990

ISBN 1 85486 014 3

Printed and bound in Great Britain by Dotesios Printers Ltd, Trowbridge, Wilts.

CONTENTS

Introduction

In this important 50th Battle of Britain anniversary year, a reissue of *Scale Models* magazine's most popular and widely-acclaimed 'special' – Aircraft from the Battle of Britain – is particularly well timed. Amongst the enormous landslide of 1940s Battle literature, it remains as unique today as it was when first published in 1982, for there is no other title available devoted to *modelling* the famous machines which took part in the summer air war over Great Britain in 1940.

Although new model kits have come and old models gone – some to reappear again in a new guise – the kits for the 12 subject aeroplanes discussed in this book are still more or less readily obtainable, and so, apart from minor updating, revision of the original text was considered unnecessary. In recent years, the world's major kit manufacturers have returned to World War Two to produce new versions of old favourites to a quality, accuracy and detail undreamt of in years past.

Nevertheless, the model world still remains the poorer for lack of definitive kits in 1/72nd scale for the Defiant Mk1, Ju88 – *any* Ju88 – and the Blenheim MkIV. The various chapters of this book explaining how to correct and improve the chosen kits, therefore, still hold true.

Since 1982, accessory parts in white metal and brass have become increasingly available and have proven to be widely popular. Many of these items can now be employed on the projects described throughout the following pages. Happy modelling!

Ray Rimell, 1990.

Part 1
Defenders

Defiant Mk.1

Improving the Airfix Boulton Paul day fighter

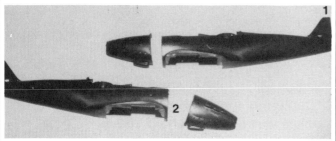

Stage 1

The big problem with the Airfix kit is the fuselage as comparison with the scale drawings reproduced alongside will reveal. Modification of the kit nose is virtually impossible and the easiest solution; mould a complete new fuselage — nevertheless, I did it the hard way. First saw off the rudder portions (1) which are mishapen, and the nose portion just forward of the wing root leading edge (2). These 'left overs' are discarded.

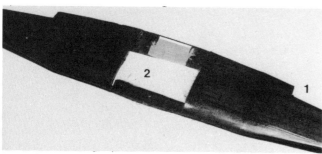

Stage 2

Assemble the kit wings, removing the ailerons in the process (1). Clean up the undercarriage cut-outs, chisel away the wing roots and add a plastic card floor (2) cementing it to the inside surfaces of the *upper* wing halves. Not only does this act as a roof for the wheel wells but also as a cockpit floor.

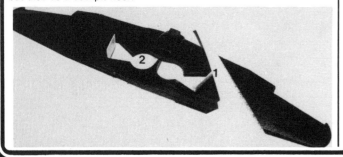

Author's completed model with Milliput and plastic card to cure some of the errors inherent in the Airfix kit.

Stage 3

Add the walls to the wheel wells from 10 thou plastic card (1). They will need to be done in several sections, are cut oversize and cemented to edges and floor (2). When thoroughly secure, the excess plastic is trimmed away and the whole wing unit sanded smooth; removing the excessive rivets at the same time.

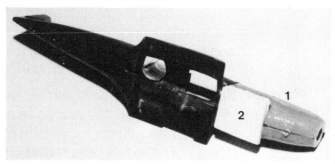

Stage 4

A new nose is now in order and we used an old **Heller** Spitfire Vb kit to obtain this item (1) packing out the wing gap with thick plastic card (2) the entire nose interior is then filled with **Milliput**. A wedge may be required to force out the Spitfire halves so they meet the width of the Defiant fuselage accurately. Ensure that all the saw cuts are precise and check constantly with the drawings for fuselage contours.

Stage 5

No cockpit detail is supplied with the Defiant and so this has to be scratchbuilt using sheet plastic and strips for side detail (1). In this view the cockpit floor is visible (2) and note how the nose has been sanded almost to final shape (3). Milliput is next applied liberally to external nose joints and left to set.

Stage 6

With all the Milliput fully set, final carving and sanding of the nose now takes place. The plastic at the extreme end may give

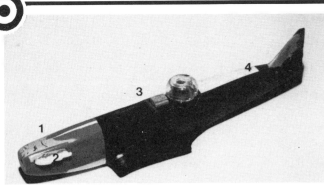

out, but the Milliput beneath will support the shape (**1**). Exhaust stacks, from spares box or plastic card, can now be installed (**2**) and a 'radio' added behind pilots seat position (**3**). The retractable fuselage decking aft of the turret was removed, and shown dropped flush by fitting a suitably scored panel of 5 thou plastic card (**4**).

Stage 7

The wings are now attached to the airframe and should be securely taped whilst the glue sets to ensure the correct attitude. Milliput or **Polyfilla** is then applied to the roots (**1**) and later smoothed in with wet n' dry paper. At this stage, an attempt was made to correct the fin with a section of plastic card and some filler (**2**). It was not at all successful and later abandoned in favour of an entirely original unit.

REFERENCES WE CONSULTED

Cockpit Data

Pilot's Notes. Boulton Paul Defiant. *From Air Data Publications. Back West Crescent, St. Annes on Sea, Lancashire.* One of scores of official reproductions taken from original AM documents. They provide invaluable illustration and data to aid modellers in creating miniature cockpits.

RAF Fighters. Part 1. One of the WW2 Aircraft Fact Files published by *MacDonald and Janes.* Written by William Green and Gordon Swanborough, a large section of the book concerns the Defiant including a John Weal cutaway. Reviewed *SM December 1978.*

GENERAL DRAWINGS

Pat McCaffrey's drawings reproduced alongside are the result of careful research into official documents and study of the preserved example at Hendon. *Aviation News* plans range also includes Defiant scale drawings and profiles appear in the Green/Swanborough title. One vital reference is 'The Disappointing Defiants' by Les Whitehouse that appeared in *Air Enthusiast Five.* This well documented article detailed Defiant history and was supported by cutaway, drawings and colour side views.

Stage 8

It all happens now! With the wings firmly attached and faired in, leading edge lamps (**1**) and navigation lights (**2**) from clear and coloured sprue are attached and later sanded to follow the wing contours. New ailerons (**3**) are cut from plastic card, filed to shape and glued in.

The entire fin was sawn off, and a completely new tail unit (**4**) was scratchbuilt from plastic card, suitably shaped and scored to represent panelling, rib tapes, trim tabs, etc. The correct shapes can be transferred from the scale drawings to the plastic and cut out accordingly, elevators and rudder being cut separately so they can be affixed at different attitudes. Some Milliput will be required to fair in the new unit and to make up the fillets for fin and tailplane. All final cleaning up is completed at this stage and model primed for its colour scheme.

Painting

The model represents PS-Z (L7029) a Mk1 of 204 Squadron and finished in the standard scheme for the period — refer to Neil Robinson's text and drawings for alternative schemes and details of colours. All roundels, fin flashes and codes were courtesy of the **Letraset** ranges and the serial was made up from digits on **Modeldecal** sheet No. 33.

Stage 9

Prior to painting, a new nose scoop (from scrap plastic) is added to the underside (**1**), and a new radiator flap from thin sheet (**2**) Also the 'straps' at the wing dihedral breaks which are fashioned from thin sprue floated on with liquid cement (**3**). Note the additional braces to the undercarriage legs (**4**) and replacement wheels from the scrap box (**5**). Find a new airscrew while you're about it — I think mine was from yet another Spitfire — all those kits have a use after all!

Stage 10

In its camouflage finish, the remodelled Defiant takes on a more convincing appearance. Final modifications and additions include a new cockpit canopy (1), new guns from sprue (2), replacement tailwheel (3), undercarriage doors from plastic card (4), and canopy framing from painted decal strip. The underfuselage aerials are from

COLOURS

The aforementioned *RAF Fighters* is a useful reference to Defiant schemes. Best reference of all is **Ducimus Camouflage and Markings No. 8** by the late 'Bob' Jones includes reliable colour and camouflage details as well as many useful photographs. Reviewed SM *June 1971*.

Acknowledgements

For help in the preparation of this feature I would like to express my thanks to Messrs. L. Whitehouse and P. McCaffrey.

(1) Defiant Mk.I, L7013, PS.U of No. 264 Squadron, circa June 1940. L7013 is an example of an aircraft initially being delivered with Night/White undersurfaces and 42-inch Type A fuselage roundels — the narrow Yellow outer ring being added in May 1940 (together with the introduction of fin stripes), and the under-surfaces repainted in Sky early in June. Code letters, PS appeared in front of the roundel on both sides of the fuselage. B scheme pattern. (2) Defiant Mk.I, believed to be L7009, TW.H of No. 141 Squadron, July 1940. Crewed by Flt. Lt. I. Donald (pilot) and Plt. Off. Hamilton (gunner), L7009 was shot down by Bf 109E's of II/JG 2, on 19th July 1940. It is thought that this machine carried a cartoon cockerel on the port fuselage under the windscreen, with the legend "cock of the North", but details are obscure. Code letters TW appeared in front of the roundel on both sides of the fuselage. B Scheme pattern.

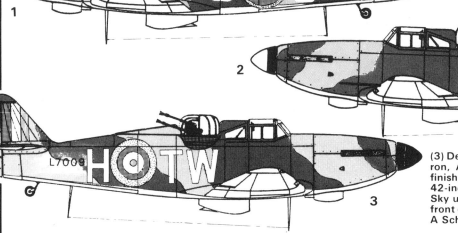

(3) Defiant Mk.I, L7026, PS.V of No. 264 Squadron, August 1940. Standard 'Battle of Britain' finish, with 24-inch wide full height fin strips, 42-inch Type A1 production style roundel and Sky under surfaces. Code letters PS appeared in front of the roundel on both sides of the fuselage. A Scheme pattern.

sprue and note that rear one is semi-retractable.

Camouflage and markings

FINISHED in Dark Green, (Humbrol HB1 plus a dash of Red No. 60), and Dark Earth, (Humbrol HB2), uppersurfaces, in one of two standard camouflage patterns, referred to as A and B schemes, up until June 1940 the undersurfaces were painted Night (black) on the port, and White on the starboard, invariably divided equally down the aircraft's centreline. In June, this undersurface scheme was changed to overall Sky, (Humbrol HB5).

Immediately before the evacuation of France in March 1940, markings had been set for 56 inch diameter Type B upperwing roundels, with 42-inch Type A fuselage roundels. As No. 264 Squadron, (at that time the only operational Defiant Squadron), was heavily involved as fighter cover for channel convoys, underwing Type A roundels were also carried, following an Air Ministry order stipulating underwing roundels to be worn by all RAF aircraft operating over or near the French mainland. Fin stripes and the Yellow outer ring to the fuselage roundels were introduced during May. 8 inch wide stripes extending the full height of the fin were applied with few deviations but the Yellow outer ring to the fuselage roundel was subject to various interpretations, such as increasing the roundel size to 58.8 inch diameter by the addition of an 8.4 inch wide Yellow outer ring, a narrower Yellow outer ring of some 2 to 3 inches width, or the correct repainting of the roundel with revised dimensions to create a 42 inch diameter Type A1 marking. Spinners were painted in Night, with the nose cap in White, an anomaly that seems to be peculiar to No. 204 Squadron. The framing to the dorsal turret was also painted Night, but this was a feature that appears to be common on all Defiants.

In mid-July 1940, a second Defiant Squadron, No. 141, was formed, which followed the same camouflage and markings practices as No. 264 with the possible exception of having all black spinners — perhaps a reader can clarify this point?

By early August, it was becoming increasingly apparent that as a day fighter the Defiant's days were numbered, and both Squadrons gradually turned over to night fighter patrols — still wearing their day fighter camouflage schemes. The height of the fin stripes had been standardised at 27 inches on 1st August, effectively produced by painting out the top portion of the stripes in the appropriate camouflage colour on in-Squadron machines, and delivered with the revised standard dimensions on new aircraft.

In late October/early November 1940, with the Defiant's duties now almost entirely confined to night operations, both active Squadrons and those in the process of forming, began to adopt the overall black RDM2A Special Night finish, (Humbrol No. 33 Matt Black as a base/undercoat, with one coat of Pelican Plaka Matt Black water based paint as a top coat). No. 204 Squadron's White spinner caps disappeared, and in an effort to further tone down any light areas on the aircraft, the Red and Blue portions of the fuselage roundels were increased to obliterate the White.

Reduction of the width of the Yellow outer ring to either a narrow band, or even completely painted out, was also recorded on certain aircraft. Fin stripes however appear to have been retained in their production form, without any modification.

Until the adoption of the all black night fighter scheme, serial numbers were presented in 8 inch high Night characters, positioned just in front of and slightly lower than the tailplane leading edge. With the application of the RDM2A finish, the serial numbers were repainted in Dull Red. Code letters remained in Sky Grey and were generally, approximately 30 inches or so, in height.

One final feature, only apparent on Dark Green/Dark Earth finished Defiants, was the black outline walkway panel on the aircrafts' port wing root, which can be best reproduced with strips of black decal or Letraset.

Defiant Data

Photos: via L. Whitehouse

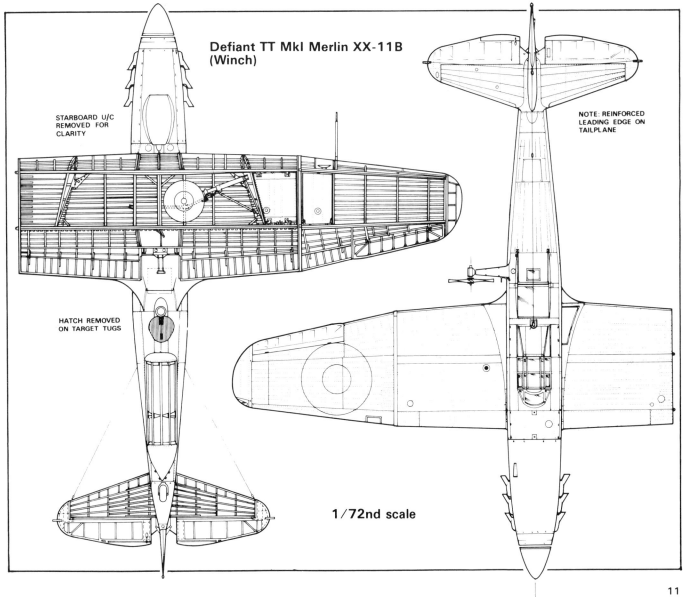

Defiant TT MkI Merlin XX-11B (Winch)

STARBOARD U/C REMOVED FOR CLARITY

NOTE: REINFORCED LEADING EDGE ON TAILPLANE

HATCH REMOVED ON TARGET TUGS

1/72nd scale

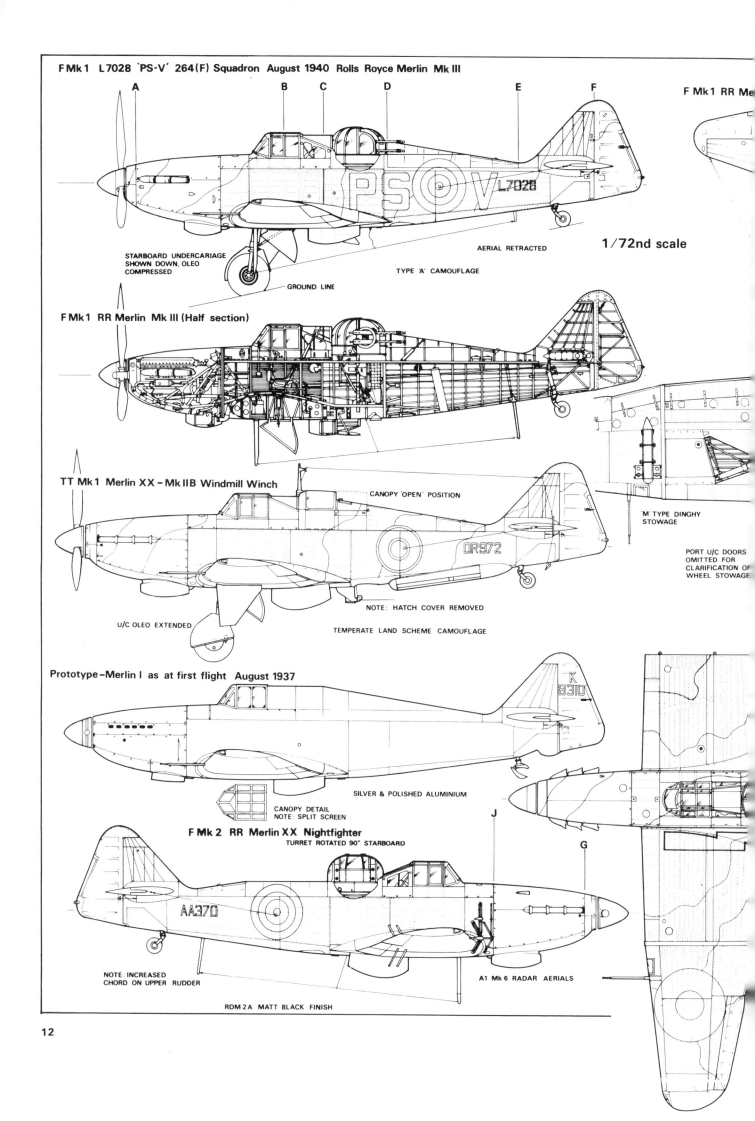

F Mk 1 L7028 'PS-V' 264(F) Squadron August 1940 Rolls Royce Merlin Mk III

A   B   C   D   E   F

F Mk 1 RR Mer

PS○V L7028

1/72nd scale

STARBOARD UNDERCARIAGE
SHOWN DOWN, OLEO
COMPRESSED

GROUND LINE

AERIAL RETRACTED

TYPE 'A' CAMOUFLAGE

F Mk 1 RR Merlin Mk III (Half section)

'M' TYPE DINGHY
STOWAGE

PORT U/C DOORS
OMITTED FOR
CLARIFICATION OF
WHEEL STOWAGE

TT Mk 1 Merlin XX – Mk IIB Windmill Winch

CANOPY 'OPEN' POSITION

DR972

U/C OLEO EXTENDED

NOTE: HATCH COVER REMOVED

TEMPERATE LAND SCHEME CAMOUFLAGE

Prototype–Merlin I as at first flight August 1937

K
8310

SILVER & POLISHED ALUMINIUM

CANOPY DETAIL
NOTE: SPLIT SCREEN

F Mk 2 RR Merlin XX Nightfighter
TURRET ROTATED 90° STARBOARD

J   G

AA370

NOTE: INCREASED
CHORD ON UPPER RUDDER

RDM 2A MATT BLACK FINISH

A1 Mk 6 RADAR AERIALS

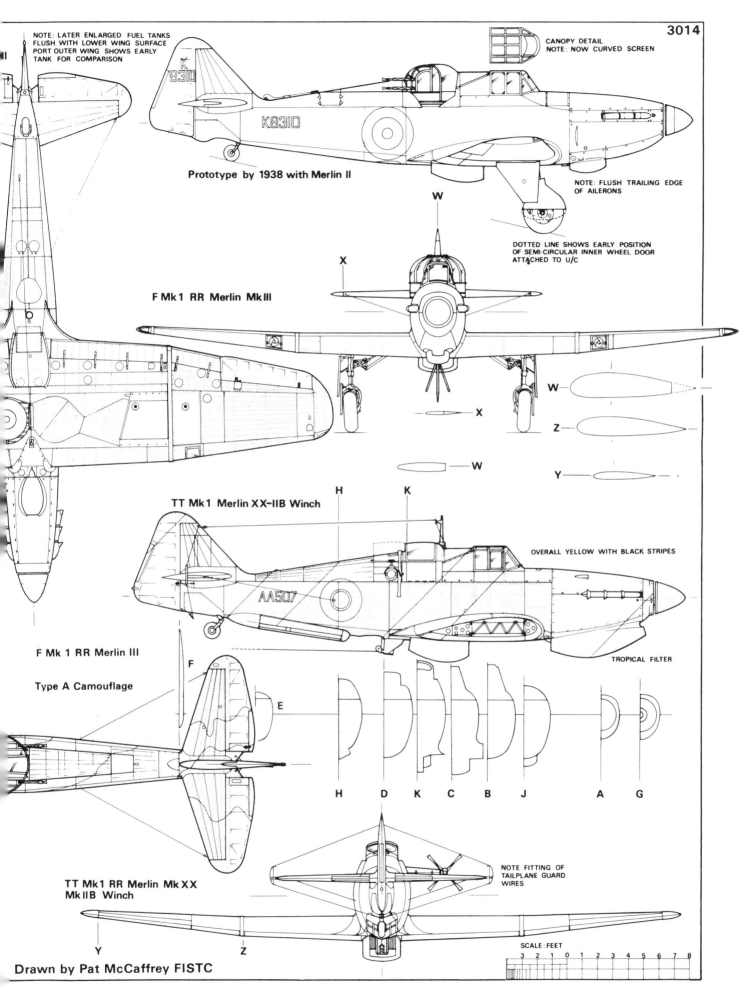

NOTE: LATER ENLARGED FUEL TANKS
FLUSH WITH LOWER WING SURFACE
PORT OUTER WING SHOWS EARLY
TANK FOR COMPARISON

CANOPY DETAIL
NOTE: NOW CURVED SCREEN

K8310

Prototype by 1938 with Merlin II

NOTE: FLUSH TRAILING EDGE
OF AILERONS

W

DOTTED LINE SHOWS EARLY POSITION
OF SEMI-CIRCULAR INNER WHEEL DOOR
ATTACHED TO U/C

X

F Mk 1 RR Merlin Mk III

W

X

Z

W

Y

TT Mk 1 Merlin XX-IIB Winch

H   K

OVERALL YELLOW WITH BLACK STRIPES

AA507

F Mk 1 RR Merlin III

TROPICAL FILTER

Type A Camouflage

F

E

H   D   K   C   B   J   A   G

TT Mk 1 RR Merlin Mk XX
Mk IIB Winch

NOTE FITTING OF
TAILPLANE GUARD
WIRES

Y   Z

SCALE: FEET
3 2 1 0 1 2 3 4 5 6 7 8

Drawn by Pat McCaffrey FISTC

Boulton Paul Defiant Mk1

Beaufighter 1F

THE pugnacious Bristol Beaufighter can justifiably be included in this series for its success as a nightfighter towards the end of the Battle when the Luftwaffe concentrated on nocturnal raids, earned it a place in the history of 1940. The Mk IF version featured here is the result of combining pieces from several kits to make just one good replica. If you thought that this would be one of the easiest models to produce in the collection you couldn't be more wrong .

STAGE 1

For the basis of the model I used the old **Frog** kit later reboxed under the **Novo** label. First the fuselage halves and wings can be assembled and left to set before any further work is carried out. Frog's engine nacelles like every other 1/72nd Beau' before or since are very poor and were replaced here with suitably modified replacements from a Frog Blenheim — an **Airfix** one will do just as nicely. (1) Fill *all* the joins, refine the gills, remove the scoops, cylinder head bumps etc before cementing the cowlings into place. A plastic card disc cemented behind each engine deals with the unrealistic open area that otherwise occurs. Cut out the raised radar housing on the nose, replace with a plastic card segment (2) and then reshape and sand flush. Cut out aileron (3) and recement at a different attitude then saw out apertures for wing tip lights (4). Also seen in our photograph is the pilot hole for the new wing intakes (5) and the sawn out section for the wing landing lamps (6).

STAGE 2

The Frog kit features the late version dihedralled tailplane and as the short span 'flat' tail is required for our model the kit parts need modifying (1). First cut off the elevators and discard, then remove ¼" section from each root before cementing flush to the model. Later new elevators are cut and shaped from plastic sheet using ASP SCALE MODELS Plan Pack as a guide to correct shapes. Add filler to all areas likely to need it, i.e. nose, sink marks in Fuselage, nacelle joints etc. (2). Finally remove the rudder, ensure the edges are cleaned up and then recement at an angle if so desired (3).

STAGE 3

The tailwheel retracted forward on Beau's and the model requires a cut out and faired in well. Drill and file away the cutout (1) and prepare a plastic sheet surround complete with floor (2) smooth off and cement into the gap. Leave about an ⅛" above the fuselage, add filler all round the lip then sand to blend into the fuselage. Study of photos reveals that the wheel well sides form an extended surround and are not flush with the fuselage. In our picture one of the new elevators (3) can be seen.

STAGE 4

The new wing intakes, seemingly undersized on all Beau' kits are tricky to install. I used old bomb casings suitably shaped and drilled (1) and then cemented into the leading edge. A large enough hole is drilled in the wing first to accommodate the new intake and care is needed not to split open the wing joint (2) while doing this. The casing is slipped into the aperture and firmly glued before hiding the joints later.

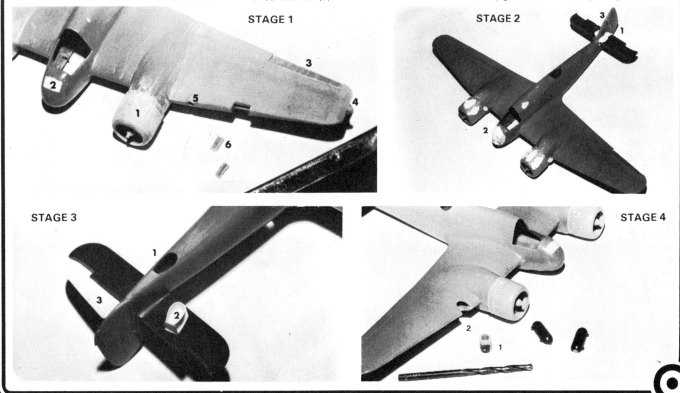

STAGE 1

STAGE 2

STAGE 3

STAGE 4

STAGE 5

Drill out all machine gun positions in wing leading edges (1) and the cannon troughs in the nose (2). Using coloured and clear sprue add the wing tip lights (3) firmly gluing into place and later these are filed down to match the tip contours. Cockpit detail is perfectly possible to add from beneath and through the cockpit before finally gluing in the fuselage belly pan. I fitted out the interior with bulkheads, floor, seats, entry hatches, side consoles etc using the cutaway as a guide and the **Air Data** publication on the Beaufighter. Don't forget to cut out the slot (4) for the access ladder on the forward hatch blanking off the inside with a layer of plastic sheet. Note here that the landing lamp aperture has been faced with sheet (5) and sanded smooth to the wing. It also helps to add a location tab at the rear of the fuselage to support the under panel (6) when this is detached later.

STAGE 6

Here the tailwheel well has been trimmed and filled (1) and the belly panel firmly glued (2). Note recess for the access hatch ladder (3) in which, after the assembly has dried thoroughly, the ladder itself can be added from stretched sprue.

STAGE 7

Before the model can be given a coat of primer, certain other modifications need to be undertaken. Such refinements include reshaping and trimming the upper nacelle intakes (1) by blanking off their undersides then smoothing round all four corners to form a more oval appearance. An additional smaller scoop was fitted to the extreme rear of each intake (sketch A) and are easily fabricated from scrap rod. Other points to remember include extending the

flap line onto the fuselage moulded wing roots from the wing undersurfaces themselves (refer to scale drawings), and adding trim tabs to each aileron. These can be sawn out and plastic sheet replacements added but note the port tab is of greater chord and is not flush with the trailing edge. At this stage the shell case ejector slots can be drilled and filed out from the wing undersides and fuselage belly.

STAGE 8

Next add the small flaps (1) beyond the new wing intakes using slivers of 10 thou plastic card, then from sprue add two breather tubes (2) to the front of each exhaust pipe (from the "MATCHBOX" kit if desired) a kit which also yields up the airscrews and spinners. The latter need modification by sanding their tips to a more blunted shape and removing at least $\frac{1}{8}$" from their rear edge. Sketch A reveals that blanking discs of plastic sheet were required to back the open spinners once they had been attached to the airscrews. (3) Our photo shows some of the added cockpit detail (4) mostly built up from plastic sheet and scrap. Behind the seat is to be found the front spar passing through each wing root and mounted atop this the rectangular 'step over' plate. Seat straps are Khaki painted draughting tape.

PAINTING

Once the model has been finally prepared, sanded, filled, smoothed *et al*, it was given two coats of **Gloy** matt black enamel serving as a primer. Over this later went another two coats, but this time **Pelikan Plaka** mixing a little white in with the black to reduce its starkness. This medium represents the original finish of Special Night (RDM 2) rather well. The model is painted overall in thin black in-

cluding the cockpit area, although fuselage and wheel well interiors were painted Aircraft Grey Green. Collector rings and exhaust pipes are a dull bronze colour.

National markings were taken from **Letraset** sheets **M9** and **M11** while the Sky Grey codes were painted on as rough squares using **Humbrol** *HX5 Light Aircraft Grey* plus a dash of *23/M8 Duck Egg Blue*. I could only locate codes of the correct size from **Letraset** sheet **M14** and being in red these were applied over the grey areas to act as a stencil. Having applied the Plaka mix over them, tape was rubbed over the area and pulled off once the paint had dried to reveal perfect codes in the correct colour. Serial number was in dull red and can be 'manufactured' in the same way if unavailable elsewhere.

The model represents T4368 a Mk IF of No 604 Squadron in the autumn of 1940 and at least one source quotes that the aircraft letter 'F' appears as a small digit on the nose. I've yet to confirm its location and if any reader can help out please can they do so in order that it can be added to the model with confidence before it goes to Hendon.

STAGE 9

Undercarriage legs as provided by Frog/Novo are rather crude and I removed the ribbing and reduced the length of the legs to match the scale drawings. The wheels lack hub detail so these were drilled out and replaced with Airfix Blenheim hubs (1), they are further improved by flattening the 'tyres' with a hot knife (2). In the photo above note also the shell case slots (3) and the belly centre line aerial from sprue (4).

STAGE 10

Drill pilot holes for the wing mounted aerials (1) AS MK IV radar, and note that

STAGE 5

STAGE 6

STAGE 7

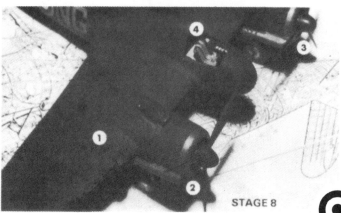

STAGE 8

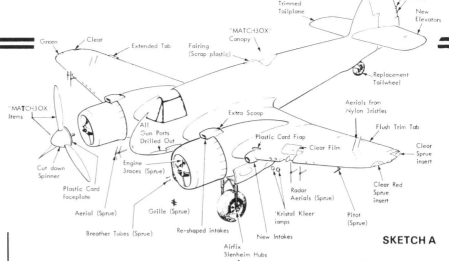

SKETCH A

here upper wing aerials are already glued in place (2). These fine nylon bristles (from an old toothbrush) are glued with PVA and are surprisingly resilient to knocks. Leading edge lamps (3) are **Kristal Kleer** blobs and the cover (thin cellophane) later attached with clear varnish then touched up with Plaka. All other aerials are made up from stretched sprue as are the 'vanes' to the leading edge intakes, the pilot tube (with a plastic card body) and rear undercarriage door and leg braces. See Sketch A to reaffirm all these modifications. Some may consider my suggestions wasteful, but I do not necessarily advocate the purchase of about four kits to make one, I just happened to have the spares at my disposal. Modellers will choose from their own scrap box or fabricate from scratch as the situation demands.

Final Suggestions

Cockpit canopy framing is painted before installation and then rear rudder lamps can be added from daubs of Kristal Kleer. Add trim tab horns and rods on tail surfaces using scrap and sprue before final touching up with the base colour as required. Drybrush Earth around wheels and undercarriage legs for a final fling and the model is now as complete as the small scale warrants . . .

REFERENCES WE CONSULTED

COCKPIT DETAIL

Pilot's Notes, Beaufighter II. *From Air Data Publications, Back West Crescent, St Annes on Sea, Lancashire.* One of scores of official reproductions taken from original AM documents. They provide invaluable illustration and data to aid modellers in creating miniature cockpits.

RAF Fighters Part 1. First of the WW2 Aircraft Fact Files published by *MacDonald and Janes.* Written by William Green and Gordon Swanborough, a large section of this book devotes itself to the Beaufighter with a Mk1 cutaway by John Weal providing useful interior detail references. Reviewed SM *December* 1978.

GENERAL DRAWINGS

One of the best available Beaufighter scale drawings can be found in the SCALE MODELS plans range. Geoff Duval's drawings are available as Plan Pack 2958. The drawings provide all necessary details for most marks and David Jones provides cutaways and cockpit drawings.

MODELLING

Beaufighter modelling data, concerned with **Revell's** 1/32nd scale kit appeared in the *May* and *July* 1974 issues of SM where Geoff Duval's drawings were originally published. Also highly recommended is the article by Neil Robinson that appeared in **Pam News No.19.** Here one can find exhaustive modelling notes and data on building, improving and converting the three available 1/72nd scale Beaufighter kits. I freely acknowledge constant reference to this feature whilst building the model shown here.

COLOURS

The aforementioned RAF Fighters Part 1 and the late Bob Jones' text found in the Beau' Plan Pack can be firmly recommended as a source for photos and colour schemes. Perhaps the best reference of all though is the **Ducimus Camouflage and Markings No 9** by James Goulding which includes reliable colour and camouflage details plus many useful reference photographs. (Reviewed *SM June* 1971).

COLOURS AND MARKINGS

DESIGNED as a long-range heavy fighter, the early marks of the Beaufighter are perhaps best remembered for their nightfighting activities, but the first Beaufighters to enter RAF service, during early September 1940 were delivered in the day fighter camouflage of Dark Green *(Humbrol HB1* Dark Green plus a dash of Red No. 60) and Dark Earth *(Humbrol HB2* Dark Earth) uppersurfaces, in one of two standard camouflage patterns, referred to as A and B schemes, with Sky *(Humbrol HB5* Sky) undersurfaces.

Upperwing roundels were Type B of 63" diameter, fuselage roundels were Type A1 of 35" diameter and underwing roundels were Type A of 45" diameter. Initially, fin stripes extending the full height of the fin and consisting of 12" wide Blue and White bars angled forward to follow the upper rudder hinge line, with the remaining portion of the fin front in Red were carried, but the standard fin flash of three 8" wide Red, White and Blue bars, 27" in height, introduced from 1st August 1940, had started to replace them by the aircraft's Squadron working-up period during the autumn of 1940. Code letters were Medium Sea Grey, serial number and propeller blades and spinners in Night (black).

The aircraft's twin engine layout, two crew accommodation, endurance, size — enough to carry the bulky early type Airborne Interception radar sets — *and* devastating armament of four 20mm cannons and six 0.303" machine guns, plus a creditable performance, made it an ideal and much needed successor to the Blenheim Mk.1F night-fighter.

The first night operations, during September and October 1940, were made in Dark Green/Dark Earth/Sky finished Beaufighters, but in late November, just after the first successful night interception by an A.I. equipped Beaufighter on the night of 19th/20th November, when a Ju 88 was destroyed by Flt/Lt John Cunningham and his A.I operator Sgt. J. Phillipson, in R2098 of No. 604 Sqdn., it was ordered that all night fighters should be painted in overall Special Night (R.D.M.2).

Code letters remained in Medium Sea Grey, but the serial numbers were changed from Night to Dull Red. Underwing roundels were not ordered to be carried on night-fighters, although because of a misunderstanding, several in-Squadron machines did retain them for some months.

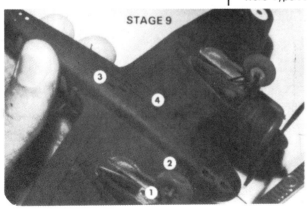

STAGE 9

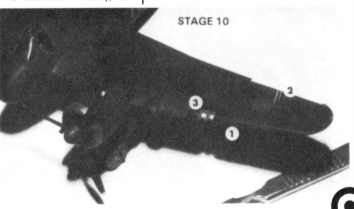

STAGE 10

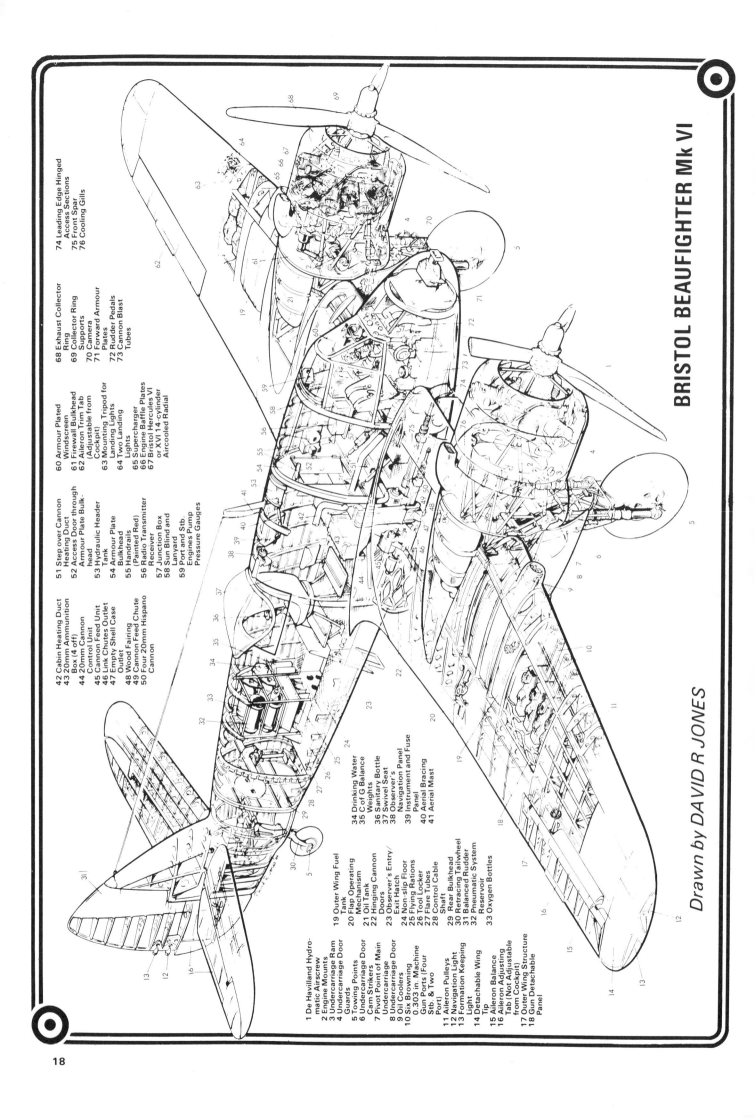

BRISTOL BEAUFIGHTER Mk VI

Drawn by DAVID R JONES

1 De Havilland Hydromatic Airscrew
2 Engine Mounts
3 Undercarriage Ram
4 Undercarriage Door Guards
5 Towing Points
6 Undercarriage Door
7 Pivot Point of Main Undercarriage
8 Undercarriage Door
9 Oil Coolers
10 Six Browning 0.303 in. Machine Gun Ports (Four Stb. & Two Port)
11 Aileron Pulleys
12 Navigation Light
13 Formation Keeping Light
14 Detachable Wing Tip
15 Aileron Balance
16 Aileron Adjusting Tab (Not Adjustable from Cockpit)
17 Outer Wing Structure
18 Gun Detachable Panel

19 Outer Wing Fuel Tank
20 Flap Operating Mechanism
21 Oil Tank
22 Hinging Cannon Doors
23 Observer's Entry/ Exit Hatch
24 Non-slip Floor
25 Flying Rations
26 Tool Locker
27 Flare Tubes
28 Control Cable Shaft
29 Rear Bulkhead
30 Retracing Tailwheel
31 Balanced Rudder
32 Pneumatic System Reservoir
33 Oxygen Bottles

34 Drinking Water Tank
35 C of G Balance Weights
36 Sanitary Bottle
37 Swivel Seat
38 Observer's Navigation Panel
39 Instrument and Fuse Panel
40 Aerial Bracing
41 Aerial Mast

42 Cabin Heating Duct
43 20mm Ammunition Box (4 off)
44 20mm Cannon Control Unit
45 Cannon Feed Unit
46 Link Chutes Outlet
47 Empty Shell Case Outlet
48 Wood Fairing
49 Cannon Feed Chute
50 Four 20mm Hispano Cannon

51 Step over Cannon Heating Duct
52 Access Door through Armour Plate Bulkhead
53 Hydraulic Header Tank
54 Armour Plate Bulkhead
55 Handrails (Painted Red)
56 Radio Transmitter Receiver
57 Junction Box
58 Sun Blind and Lanyard
59 Port and Stb. Engines Pump Pressure Gauges

60 Armour Plated Windscreen
61 Firewall Bulkhead
62 Aileron Trim Tab (Adjustable from Cockpit)
63 Mounting Tripod for Landing Lights
64 Two Landing Lights
65 Supercharger
66 Engine Baffle Plates
67 Bristol Hercules VI or XVI 14-cylinder Aircooled Radial

68 Exhaust Collector Ring
69 Collector Ring
70 Camera
71 Forward Armour Plates
72 Rudder Pedals
73 Cannon Blast Tubes

74 Leading Edge Hinged Access Sections
75 Front Spar
76 Cooling Gills

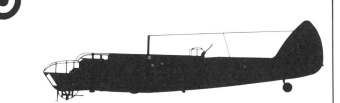

Blenheim Mk.IV

Building the big Blenheim from Airfix and Frog kits

PERHAPS one of the most well known of British Second World War twins the Blenheim is assured of a high place in the annals of RAF history and while the Mk 1 is more representative of the Battle the excellent and late-lamented **Frog** kit is not widely available these days and thus the modeller is obliged to fall back on the elderly **Airfix** Mk IV. Frankly this is not one of that company's better efforts and is long overdue for retooling, nevertheless if the modeller is not afraid of a little extra work a fairly representative replica can result.

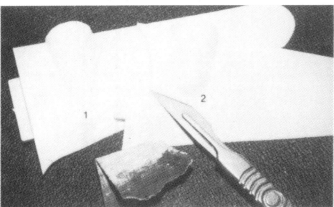

Stage 1

Perhaps the most serious fault of the Airfix Mk IV concerns the upperwing engine nacelles which are far too long. **(1)** and reference to photographs and Arthur Bentley's drawings here reveal a quite different shape. Luckily there is sufficient plastic for the modeller to hack and sand away the offending areas **(2)**. Obviously surface detail will suffer in the process, but I chose to remove it anyway later re-scribing panel lines referring to Arthur's drawings.

Stage 2

Assemble fuselage halves and wings, filling any joints that may appear. In plan view, it will be noted that the wing leading edges inboard of the nacelles taper too much towards the nacelle sides **(1)** so cut back the leading edge then fill and file to shape. Before assembly of wing halves, cut away the ailerons noting that the upper sections are

Author's model is the result of mating Frog components to the basic Airfix kit in order that a more realistic model can result. A study of the restored aircraft at Hendon is to be recommended.

narrower in chord **(2)**, dispense with the inaccurate rudder and either cut a replacement from plastic card or use a Frog kit item. The fin will need to be reshaped and here is where close reference to the drawings and photographs will really pay off, add a floor **(3)** to the cockpit area from plastic sheet and remove any remaining raised detail from the model.

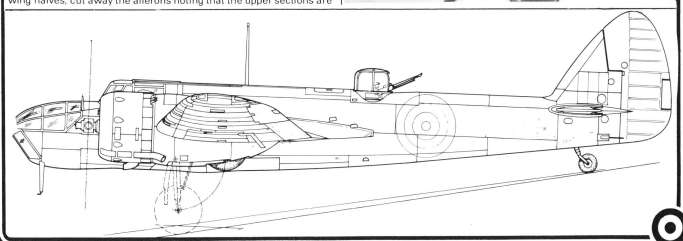

Stage 3

Frog's Mk1 engine cowling units can be used to replace the Airfix versions (**1**) and the engines are best painted prior to installation in the cowling halves. Note here the shortened nacelles (**2**) and the reworked leading edge sections immediately outboard of the fuselage (**3**). Airfix supply a bulkhead which has been resited further back here (**4**) but to be accurate it should not really appear at all. (refer to cutaway).

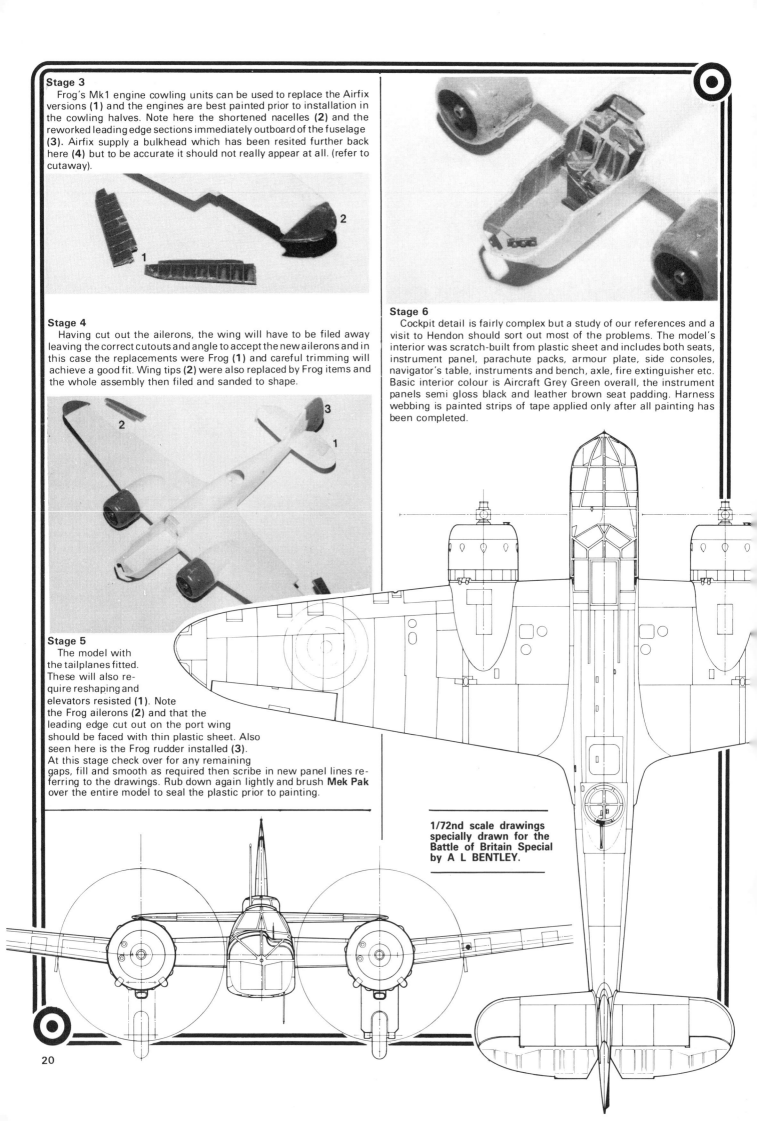

Stage 4

Having cut out the ailerons, the wing will have to be filed away leaving the correct cutouts and angle to accept the new ailerons and in this case the replacements were Frog (**1**) and careful trimming will achieve a good fit. Wing tips (**2**) were also replaced by Frog items and the whole assembly then filed and sanded to shape.

Stage 5

The model with the tailplanes fitted. These will also require reshaping and elevators resisted (**1**). Note the Frog ailerons (**2**) and that the leading edge cut out on the port wing should be faced with thin plastic sheet. Also seen here is the Frog rudder installed (**3**).
At this stage check over for any remaining gaps, fill and smooth as required then scribe in new panel lines referring to the drawings. Rub down again lightly and brush **Mek Pak** over the entire model to seal the plastic prior to painting.

Stage 6

Cockpit detail is fairly complex but a study of our references and a visit to Hendon should sort out most of the problems. The model's interior was scratch-built from plastic sheet and includes both seats, instrument panel, parachute packs, armour plate, side consoles, navigator's table, instruments and bench, axle, fire extinguisher etc. Basic interior colour is Aircraft Grey Green overall, the instrument panels semi gloss black and leather brown seat padding. Harness webbing is painted strips of tape applied only after all painting has been completed.

1/72nd scale drawings specially drawn for the Battle of Britain Special by A L BENTLEY.

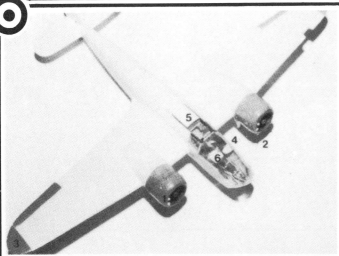

Stage 7

The model is almost ready for painting but check off the following additions first. Drill out induction pipes carried in both nacelles (1), add breather tubes from sprue in the collector rings ahead of the exhausts (2), add the wingtip lights (3). Install the canopy, after removal of the sliding hood (4) and removal of side blisters on cockpit transparencies (not all Blenheims carried these), and add hood rails from sprue (5). Fill in solid panels of nose transparency (6), add undercarriage assembles and paint interior Aircraft Grey Green. There are no wheel well walls as such and on the real aircraft one can look upright past the complex undercarriage mechanism to see the inside surface of the nacelle. How much detail one wishes to add inside the bays is a matter of choice — certainly a lot of careful sprue work will be called for. As I did not intend to display the model over a mirrored base, and copy date was pressing, I chose to eschew this extra detailing . . .

Painting

The model represents K·BL (R3744) a Mk IV of 40 Squadron circa July 1940. Refer to Neil Robinson's text for a guide to colours which were fairly typical of the period, the aircraft carrying the standard Dark Earth/Dark Green/Sky finish. All roundels, fin flashes and codes were courtesy of the **Letraset** ranges and the serial was made up from digits on **Modeldecal sheet No. 33.** Medium Grey codes are required but note that K is outlined thinly in white and there is a fairly simple method of reproducing this. Using Letraset codes firm down the letter onto white decal film, I used one of **Microscale's** new sheets, and ensure the digit is well rubbed down. Using a sharp knife simply cut out the letter but leaving a thin outline all round it and apply the decal in the normal way.

Stage 8

More details to note here. This particular aircraft, as most early Blenheim Mk IVs carried a rearward firing gun within a transparent blister. This could be moulded but I found an unused cockpit side panel from a **Tamiya** Lancaster which, with a little filing, seemed just right for the job (1). Other points are the pitot (2), venturi tube (3), sprue exhaust stubs (4), Frog airscrews (5), and drilling out of the nacelle intakes (6). Also note that the flap positions (7) have been scored in and that the 'tyres' are flattened (8).

Stage 9

Easiest way to paint the complex canopy framing is by using strips of

clear decal film (1) which are first painted Aircraft Grey Green. When perfectly dry apply a coat of Dark Earth/Dark Green over the top and later cut up into strips then apply to the transparencies with Microsol and setting aside to dry out. It is an effective method as when viewed from beneath, the green undercoat of the film gives the illusion of internally painted frames. I replaced the bomb aimer's 'window' with thin panes of clear plastic sheet (2) and the turret was carefully sanded and polished for a more realistic appearance (3). Replacement gun(s) were also found and as a final touch an aerial cable made up from stretched sprue, lamps on rudder and wing cut out were simply blobs of silver paint glazed with **Kristal Kleer.**

Final Suggestions

Obviously some compromises have been made in the creation of this model and there may be better and cheaper ways of achieving the same end result. Therefore one is advised to compare the Airfix model with Arthur Bentley's drawings before chopping and changing is commenced and decide their own route to modification. Final touches to the model included a wing walkway from dark grey decal film and faint 'weathering' round tyres and undercarriage areas using 'Light Earth'.

Ron Moulton snapped this Blenheim/Bolingbroke at Chino in 1978.

REFERENCES WE CONSULTED

COCKPIT DATA

Pilot's Notes, Blenheim Mk1 (Mk IV to be available later). *From Air Data Publications, Back West Crescent, St Annes on Sea, Lancashire.* One of scores of official reproductions taken from original AM documents. They provide invaluable illustration and data to aid modellers in creating miniature cockpits.

RAF Bombers Part 1. Another in the WW2 Aircraft Fact Files published by *MacDonald and Janes.* Written by William Green and Gordon Swanborough, a large section of the book devotes itself to the Blenheim family and includes a John Weal cutaway.

GENERAL DRAWINGS

Arthur Bentley's drawings reproduced alongside are the careful result of research into Bristol's own archives and study of the Bolingbroke that can be seen at the museum today. Scale drawings of the type are comparatively rare it seems and in the fullness of time we hope to redress the situation. **Aviation News'** plans ranges also includes drawings of the Blenheim family which were produced by R. Miller.

COLOURS

The aforementioned RAF Bombers is a useful reference to

BRISTOL BLENHEIM Mk IV

Tony Barnes

TONY BARNES 1980

22

Blenheim schemes and so is **Profile No. 218** by *James D. Oughton* now available within Volume 10 of the bound profiles. Best reference of all is **Ducimus Camouflage and Markings No. 7** by *James Goulding* which includes reliable colour and camouflage details as well as many useful photographs.

Acknowledgements

For help in the preparation of this feature I would like to express my thanks to Messrs M.A. Barnes, A.L. Bentley, P.G. Cooksley, R. Dawes and E.E. Stretch.

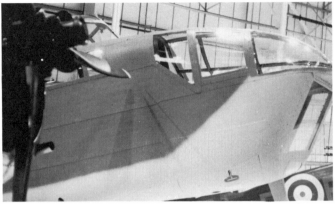

Author's pictures at RAF Hendon reveal areas of the Bleinheim that require attention by a fastidious modeller. Note in particular the under-carriage legs and engine areas, both calling out for careful sprue work for absolute authenticity.

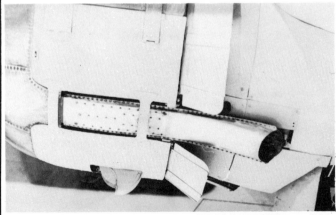

COLOURS AND MARKINGS

BEING *classed* as fighters, the Blenheim Mk. If's and IVF's adopted the current Fighter Command scheme of Dark Green (**Humbrol HB1 Dark Green** plus a dash of Red No. 60), and Dark Earth (**Humbrol HB2 Dark Earth**) uppersurfaces, in one of two standard camouflage patterns, referred to as A and B schemes, with Night (black) port and White starboard undersides, either divided equally down the centre line, or simply with the starboard wing and tailplane painted White over the original Night underside finish. Inevitably there were variations to these two underside schemes, but these were the most common. National markings followed the progressive changes, which by early 1940, had been fixed at Type B upperwing, and Type A fuselage roundels. No underwing roundels were carried, unless operations over the French mainland were undertaken, in which case a Type A1 roundel was applied under the Night port wing and a Type A under the White starboard wing. Fin stripes were not introduced until May 1940, when they were painted the full height of the fin, normally in 6 to 7 inch widths, occasionally of greater widths, and sometimes even covering the entire fin area. The Yellow outer ring to the fuselage roundels was also reinstated at this time, converting them into Type A1.

Following experiments with alternative undersurface colours during 1939, the most successful colour, Sky, was adopted in June 1940, followed in August by the general application of underwing Type A roundels.

Standardisation of these camouflage schemes and markings changes had just begun to take real effect, including a revised fin flash of three 8 inch wide Red, White and Blue stripes, 27 inches in height, when, in mid-November 1940, it was ordered that Night Fighters would be painted in Special Night (R.D.M.2) overall. As it had become patently obvious that the Blenheim fighter was totally inadequate for the type of daylight operations it was expected to contend with over the British Isles during the summer of 1940, the aircraft's twin engined layout and endurance was found to lend itself ideally to the task of Night Fighter, pending the introduction of a much more capable machine which was to result in the shape of the Beaufighter.

The comparatively roomy fuselage of the Blenheim could readily carry the new airborne night interception apparatus, and in fact a Blenheim Mk.1 of the Fighter Interception Unit at Ford had claimed the first radar assisted "kill" on the night of 2nd/3rd July 1940. It would appear that it was mainly the Blenheim Mk. IF that was painted in Special Night (R.D.M.2) and fitted with A.I radar, most of the remaining longer nosed Blenheim Mk. IVF's, being operated by Coastal Command Squadrons, where once again the type's twin engines and endurance proving useful for long range "trade protection" patrols over the North Sea, retained the standard Day Fighter scheme of Dark Green/Dark Earth/Sky. Medium Sea Grey code letters and Night serial numbers were carried in the usual positions, although some difficulty in the placing of the port side Squadron code letters was initially experienced due to the standard forward location of the fuselage roundel near to the wing root trailing edge fillet, resulting in the roundel being moved further aft on some machines. With the introduction of the overall Special Night (R.D.M.2) finish, the serial number was repainted in Dull Red, but the code letters remained in Medium Sea Grey.

Gladiator II

Gloster's immortal biplane fighter — how to improve the Heller kit

AS FK Mason says in his superb book *'Battle over Britain'* the Gladiator was 'an anachronistic survival from an earlier generation of fighter aircraft. Nevertheless it was a magnificent aircraft, and the damage it was to inflict for many months after the close of the battle qualify it for inclusion in any review of the equipment with which Fighter Command faced the onslaughts of 1940'.

What more needs to be said other than that the subject kit for this month's feature is **Heller's**.

Completed model as HPB of 247 Squadron and finished in four-shade upper surface camouflage colours apparently rare in that squadron — but does anyone have *reliable* patterns for the normal Dk Earth/Green scheme?

Stage 1.

First job is to remove all internal fuselage pegs, ledges, etc., and then the rudder. (**1**) so that it can later be reattached at a different attitude. Also carefully separate elevators and tailplanes for the same reason. (**2**) Cockpit detail can be added from scrap and sprue although Heller supply a fair amount themselves. Check out the list of references at the end of this feature for further cockpit data.

Stage 2.

Join fuselage halves and apply filler to upper fuselage joins where it may be needed (**1**). Assemble control panel to the forward fuselage section and clean up all mating edges (**2**). Some of the Heller cockpit detail can just be seen (**3**).

Stage 3.

I found a spare "**MATCHBOX**" Gladiator engine which somehow looked much more realistic than Heller's offering and installed it accordingly (**1**). Next the Heller cowling was assembled together and the trailing edges pared and sanded to a wafer thin setion (**2**). An airscrew for Mk II versions is supplied by Heller but very crude, a Swordfish kit yielded my replacement (**3**) which was cut down to size and considerable time was spent filing and sanding the blades as thin as possible. Actually it should be a Watts two-blader!

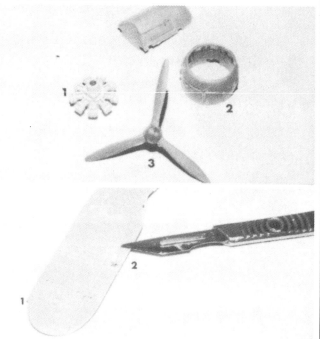

Stage 4.

Cut off the wing tip 'lights' (**1**) moulded with the upper wing which are moulded solid and can be improved. Another modification concerns the flaps which were reamed out on my model by careful scraping with a sharp craft knife (**2**). Later clean up and score in faint lines to represent ribbing.

Stage 5.

Assembly of the lower wing to the fuselage demands care and filler will be required around several joints as seen on previous page. **(1)**. The gun fairings are cemented in place **(2)** but the barrels are removed to be replaced later with sprue items. Tailplanes are cemented in place and await attachment of elevators **(3)** which should have their edges rounded before tacking in place.

Stage 6.

Cockpit interior is almost complete **(1)** and instrument panel painted and detailed **(2)** before attaching the forward section to the fuselage. Heller do provide a forward fuselage radiator matt but it is overscale and was replaced on my model with scored 5 thou card.

Stage 7.

Most of the painting was accomplished before the model was assembled and a good colour scheme can be found on page 553 of the *September* issue of SCALE AIRCRAFT MODELLING **Letraset sheets** (available from **BMW Models**) supplied the national markings (**M9** and **M11**) with **Modeldecal** providing grey codes and black serials: model is painted in the four tone shadow compensating scheme and carries sky undersides. "MATCHBOX" kit wheels have been fitted **(1)** and slight weathering effects around nose and tail surfaces. Complete the kit as per kit instructions later adding the flaps from scored sections of 5 thou plastic card.

Stage 8.

Virtually complete, the model is ready for rigging using rolled copper wire **(1)** dividers to measure lengths **(2)**, and steel ruler to roll the wire out **(3)**. Gladiator bracing wires are not too complicated and the careful modeller could complete the operation in about an hour. Final additions would be new wing guns from sprue **(4)** pitot tube from fuse wire and navigation lamps from **Kristal Kleer** tinted with food colouring. (Ignore that airscrew!)

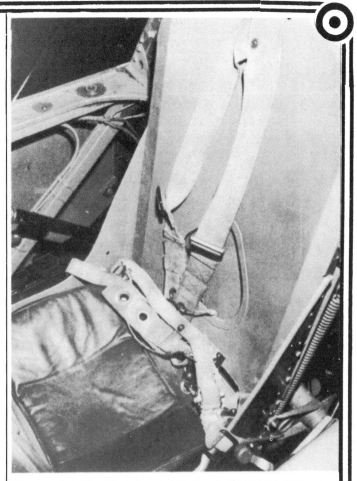

Close-up detail for Gladiator modellers — cockpit seat and harness — note leather cushion and below, that Bristol Mercury power plant — plenty of scope for stretched sprue work here!

REFERENCES WE CONSULTED

Cockpit data

Air Data Publications, Back West Crescent, St Annes on Sea, Lancashire. One of scores of official reproductions taken from original Air Ministry documents. They provide invaluable illustration data to aid modellers in creating miniature cockpits.

RAF Fighters Part 1 First of the WW2 Aircraft Fact Files published by *MacDonald and Janes.* Written by William Green and Gordon Swanborough, a section of the book devotes itself to the Gladiator with a cutaway by John Weal providing useful interior detail references. Reviewed SM *December* 1978.

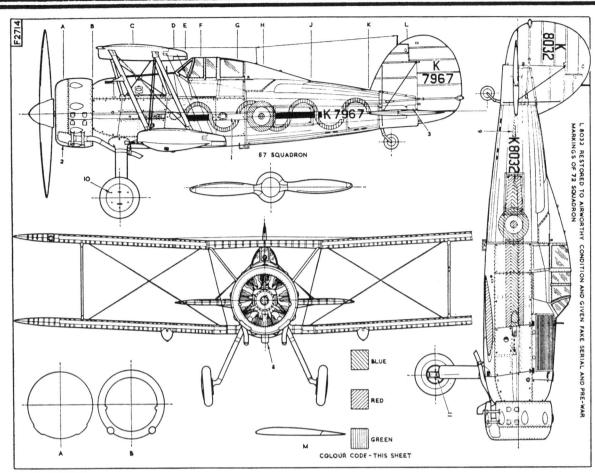

1/72nd scale drawings by G. A. G. COX

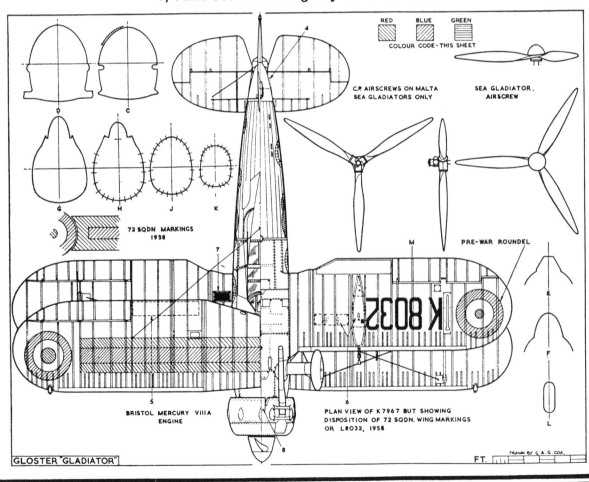

GLOSTER "GLADIATOR"

General drawings

One of the best available Gladiator scale drawings can be found in the SCALE MODELS Plans range. George Cox's drawings are available as Plan Pack 2714. The plan pack contains plenty of details and many photographs of the cockpit layout.

Modelling

Gladiator modelling features have appeared several times within these pages. Check out SM *August* 1973 issue for modelling notes on the kit, and article which included colour plates, scale drawings and plenty of photographs. An aerobatic team was also described in the *October* 1978 issue where we showed how to super-detail the ''MATCHBOX'' kit.

Colours

The aforementioned RAF Fighters Part 1 can be recommended as a source for photographs and a little colour data, then there is **Profile Publication No. 95** (In *Volume 5)* and the superb **Ducimus flage and Markings No. 5** which includes reliable data on Gladiator colours and camouflage colours and camouflage details. (Reviewed SM *January,* 1971).

Completed model fully rigged and detailed. Surprisingly, the Gladiator has proven the easiest model to construct of our series. Sprue doubles for wing guns, rigging 'acorns', and fin aerial mast. Cockpit hood slid back to view interior detail and canted tailwheel add touches of realism.

COLOURS AND MARKINGS

AS No. 247 Squadron was the only Gladiator equipped front line unit in RAF Fighter Command during the Battle of Britain, this month's camouflage and markings notes can be specifically related to this unit alone.

Formed from the Sumburgh Fighter Flight, based in the Shetlands, No. 247 Squadron was re-formed at Roborough, Devon, on 1st August 1940 and became operational on 13th August, (with additional aircraft from No. 152 Squadron which had re-equipped with Spitfires), flying from Roborough during the day, primarily in the defence of Plymouth, and spending the night at readiness at St. Eval, Cornwall.

Despite the promulgation of the four tone shadow compensating

Shuttleworth's Mk1 Gladiator during overhaul reveals rarely seen detail of this classic biplane's innards.

uppersurface camouflage scheme, that had been specially devised by the Royal Aircraft establishment (RAE) at Farnborough in 1939 for biplanes — consisting of Dark Green *(Humbrol* HB1 Dark Green), Dark Earth *(Humbrol* HB2 Dark Earth), and Light Earth (4 parts *Humbrol* HB2 × 1 part 34/M10 White); the lighter shades to be applied to areas on the aircraft that were theoretically in shade, such as the lower mainplanes, lower sides of the fuselage, and the fin and rudder — conversation with an eye witness who was then, and still is, a well respected aircraft modeller, would indicate that all No. 247's Gladiators were finished merely in Dark Green/Dark Earth uppersurfaces in the standard pattern then applied to Gladiators.

Sky *(Humbrol* HB5 Sky) undersurfaces were introduced in early June 1940, so by the time No. 247 Squadron was formed in August, it would seem safe to assume that this unit's machines had been repainted in this colour, this assumption being borne out, once again by eye witness reports.

Unfortunately, very few photographs exist of No. 247 Squadron Gladiators, and although the code letters HP, painted in Medium Sea Grey *(Humbrol* HB6) were allocated to the unit, it is possible that not all the machines had them applied, but of those that did have them, (N2308, HP.B for example), approximately 30 inch high codes seem to have been the most common size.

From currently available records, twelve aircraft were issued to the Squadron, all Gladiator Mk. II's — N2308, N5575, N5576, N5585, N5631, N5644, N5648, N5649, N5682, N5684, N5701, and N5897. Serial numbers were in Night (black), 6 inches high, and placed on the rear fuselage just infront of the tailplane. Upperwing roundels were 40inch diameter Type B, with 35inch Type A1 fuselage roundels, (probably converted from the previous standard 25inch Type A by the addition of a 5inch wide outer yellow ring). Fin stripes appear to have been applied over the entire fin area, consisting of equal widths of Red, White and Blue. Underwing Type A roundels of approximately 40inch diameter may have been applied prior to the Squadron reforming, but it would seem more likely they were applied by Squadron personnel during early/mid August 1940, following the order of 1st August.

It was late October before the Squadron had its first combat, intercepting a He111 on the night of the 28th but without result. In view of No. 247's imminent re-equipment with the Hurricane Mk. 1, which took place in December, and its primary role as a day fighter unit, it is very doubtful if the Squadron made any concession to its then secondary activities of night fighting by adopting any form of night fighter camouflage.

Although outside the scope of these notes, it may be of interest to modellers to know that at least two other U.K. based units operated Gladiators during the summer of 1940; No. 239 Squadron, then an Army Co-operation unit, and No. 804 Squadron, a temporarily shore based Fleet Air Arm Squadron equipped with the navalised version of the Gladiator, the Sea Gladiator.

Hurricane MK1

Detailing the most recent 1/72nd scale Airfix kit

Above and below: author's model based on the Airfix Hurricane in the markings of 17(F) Squadron, June 1940. The markings are a mixture of Letraset, Modeldecal and some careful free-style painting.

Stage 1

Without a doubt this was the easiest of all the 12 models built for the Battle series. Thanks to general accuracy and ease of assembly, I restricted the work to extra detailing and adding separated flaps. The cockpit walls were thinned down, emergency hatch cut out (1) the internal fuselage walls detailed with stretched sprue lengths (2) and a new instrument panel from 10 thou plastic card installed. Tailplane components were next to be fitted having removed the elevators (3) and then re-cemented at a 'parked' attitude.

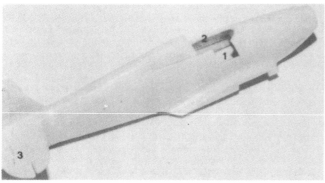

Stage 2

In order to rework the flaps, first separate the ailerons from the wings (1) and cut out the flap areas from the one piece lower wing half (2). Remove all 'tabs' from the inner lips of the undercarriage wheel wells (3).

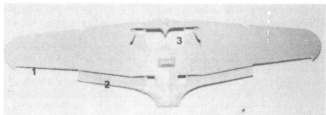

Stage 3

Test fit the wing assembly to that of the fuselage (1) and some filler may be required at the rear joint. As can be seen, the rudder has been removed then reattached (2) and the trim tab cut away for later replacement with plastic sheet.

Stage 4

Once the wing/fuselage assembly has finally dried, attach the radiator bath (1) and face the flap areas with scored 10 thou card (2) The wheel well areas are later blanked off with a section of the same material and 'walls' added later.

Stage 5

Assembly progresses. The sliding hood **(1)** has its origins in Heller's kit but if an open configuration is required then the rear fuselage behind the cockpit will have to be filed down to accept the transparency. Note the new seat **(2)** from an Airfix Spitfire and additional cockpit detailing from sprue.

Stage 6

The uppersurface is now given a coat of **Humbrol** Dark Earth prior to application of the camouflage pattern. The chosen subject is YB-W P3878 of No. 17 (F) Squadron, June 1940. This unit's machines were unusual in that several sported variations from standard markings. YB-W for example has a sky spinner, wavy demarcation line on wing leading edges and forward fuselage plus 'thickened' YB characters. The national insignia for the model came again, from **Letraset** ranges. Serials were from **Modeldecal** sheet No. 33. YB codes were also Letraset but painted over to achieve the more blocky style of the originals.

Stage 7

In this view the model is virtually complete after the addition of several details. The flaps **(1)** are cut from scored 10 thou card, additional undercarriage struttage from sprue **(2)**, and amber lamp **(3)** to rear of radiator from polished stretched sprue.

Stage 8

More details have been added. Wing walks **(1)** from black decal, cockpit mirror **(2)** from sprue, aerial cables **(3)** from sprue and painted patches **(4)** over the gun ports. Seat harness has been added to the cockpit, this from painted tape.

REFERENCES WE CONSULTED

Pilot's Notes, Hawker Hurricane 11A and IV. *Air Data Publications, Back West Crescent, St Annes on Sea, Lancashire.* One of scores of official reproductions taken from AM documents. They provide invaluable illustration and data to aid modellers in creating cockpits.

RAF Fighters Part 2. Another in the *WW2 Aircraft Fact Files* published by *MacDonald and Janes.* Written by William Green and Gordon Swanborough, a large section of the book is devoted to the Hurricane. Reviewed SM *March* 1980.

Ducimus Camouflage and Markings No. 3 by James Goulding takes the honours for colour reference, including as it does reliable camouflage details and many useful photographs. Reviewed SM *January* 1971.

COLOURS AND MARKINGS

HURRICANES entered combat finished in Dark Green *(HUMBROL HB1 Dark Green + dash of HUMBROL No. 60 Red),* and Dark Earth *(HUMBROL HB2 Dark Earth)* uppersurfaces, ine one of two standard camouflage patterns, referred to as A and B schemes. The uppersurfaces followed the normal practice of being divided centrally down the centreline in Night (black) port and White starboard for in-service repainted machines, ot, Night port wing and White starboard wing with the nose underside, rear fuselage and tailplanes in Aluminium paint (4 parts *HUMBROL* HB14 Silver + 1 part *HUMBROL* 64/M13 Light Grey), for newly delivered factory finishing aircraft.

Underwing Type A roundels were generally carried by Hurricanes operating from, or over, the French mainland but *not normally* on U.K. based home defence fighters. With the introduction of Sky undersurfaces *(HUMBROL* HB5 Sky) in June 1940, underwing roundels were to be no longer carried, although because of many of the Hurricane Squadrons' previous major involvement over France, for which under/wing roundels *were* ordered to be carried, the changes tended to take longer to implement, and Night/White, Night/White/Aluminium undersurfaces, either with or without roundels were to be seen well after the official changeover date.

Upperwing roundels remained at 49 inch diameter Type B, with fuselage roundels being either the official standard 35 inch Type A1, or, the larger 49 inch Type A1 (previously converted from the 35 inch diameter Type A roundel of late 1939/early 1940). Fin flashes showed a wide variation. Many aircraft which had not previously carried fin stripes prior to their introduction in May 1940, adopted fin flashes in Red, White and Blue bands, of either 5 inch, 6 inch or 7-8 inch widths, although what is accepted to be the official design, generally attributed to Hawker Aircraft Ltd., consisted of 9 inch wide Blue and White bands with the rest of the forward fin in Red.

The aircraft's comparatively large area of fuselage, allowed Hurricanes greater flexibility in the size of the Medium Sea Grey Squadron code letters adopted. Approximately 36 inch high code letters appear to have been the most popular, although some Squadrons, (No. 32 for example), sported 40 inch high codes. Serial numbers were in Night 8 inch high characters, positioned on the rear fuselage.

Underwing Type A roundels were re-introduced on the Sky undersurfaces in early August 1940; 45 inch diameter being the official standard size, but in practice, initially varied from 30 inch to 50 inch.

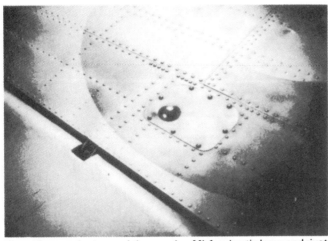

More close-up features of the genuine Mk1, wing tip lamp and rivet head variations on wing panels.

Oft-unappreciated areas of the Hurricane revealed at Hendon. Under-carriage linkage and hub, gun ports above centre line, landing lamp, and retractable step.
Photos: R. L. Rimell

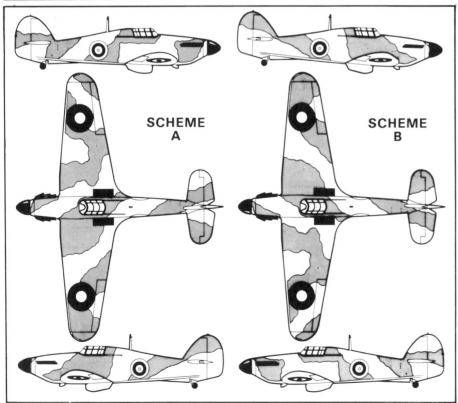

SCHEME A

SCHEME B

BASIC CAMOUFLAGE PATTERNS TINT AREAS: Dk GREEN

© A.L. BENTLEY 1980

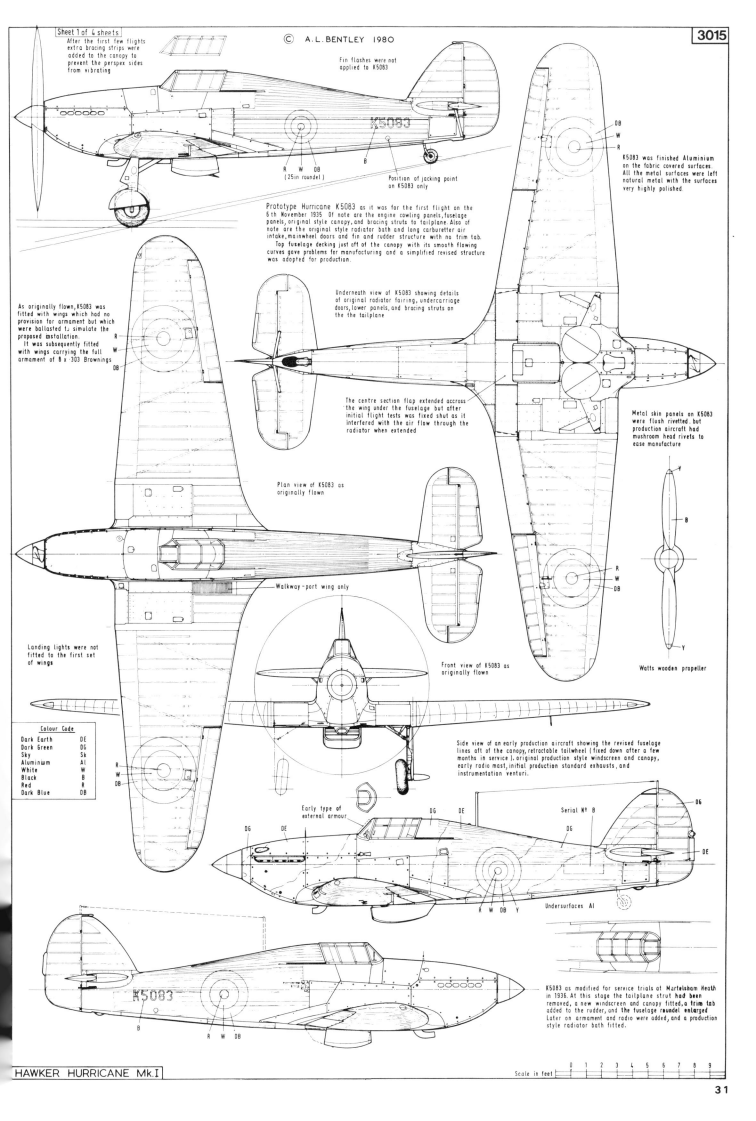

After the first few flights extra bracing strips were added to the canopy to prevent the perspex sides from vibrating

Fin flashes were not applied to K5083

K5083

R W DB
(25in roundel)

Position of jacking point on K5083 only

DB
W
R

K5083 was finished Aluminium on the fabric covered surfaces. All the metal surfaces were left natural metal with the surfaces very highly polished.

Prototype Hurricane K5083 as it was for the first flight on the 6th November 1935. Of note are the engine cowling panels, fuselage panels, original style canopy, and bracing struts to tailplane. Also of note are the original style radiator bath and long carburetter air intake, mainwheel doors and fin and rudder structure with no trim tab.
Top fuselage decking just aft of the canopy with its smooth flowing curves gave problems for manufacturing and a simplified revised structure was adopted for production.

As originally flown, K5083 was fitted with wings which had no provision for armament but which were ballasted to simulate the proposed installation.
It was subsequently fitted with wings carrying the full armament of 8 x .303 Brownings

R
W
DB

Underneath view of K5083 showing details of original radiator fairing, undercarriage doors, lower panels, and bracing struts on the the tailplane.

The centre section flap extended accross the wing under the fuselage but after initial flight tests was fixed shut as it interfered with the air flow through the radiator when extended

Metal skin panels on K5083 were flush rivetted. but production aircraft had mushroom head rivets to ease manufacture

Plan view of K5083 as originally flown

Y

B

R
W
DB

Y

Watts wooden propeller

Walkway - port wing only

Landing lights were not fitted to the first set of wings

Front view of K5083 as originally flown

R
W
DB

Colour Code	
Dark Earth	DE
Dark Green	DG
Sky	Sk
Aluminium	Al
White	W
Black	B
Red	R
Dark Blue	DB

Side view of an early production aircraft showing the revised fuselage lines aft of the canopy, retractable tailwheel (fixed down after a few months in service), original production style windscreen and canopy, early radio mast, initial production standard exhausts, and instrumentation venturi.

Early type of external armour

DG
DE

DG
DE

DG

Serial Nº B

DG

DE

Undersurfaces Al

R W DB Y

K5083

B

R W DB

K5083 as modified for service trials at Martelsham Heath in 1936. At this stage the tailplane strut had been removed, a new windscreen and canopy fitted, a trim tab added to the rudder, and the fuselage roundel enlarged. Later on armament and radio were added, and a production style radiator bath fitted.

HAWKER HURRICANE Mk.I

Scale in feet   0 1 2 3 4 5 6 7 8 9

© A.L. BENTLEY 1980

Hurricane Mk I V6864 flown by Sqdn. Ldr. Stanford Tuck D.S.O., D.F.C.
N° 257 Squadron North Weald autumn 1940. NOTE :- The camouflage pattern shown on
Tucks aircraft is the scheme B "mirror image" pattern

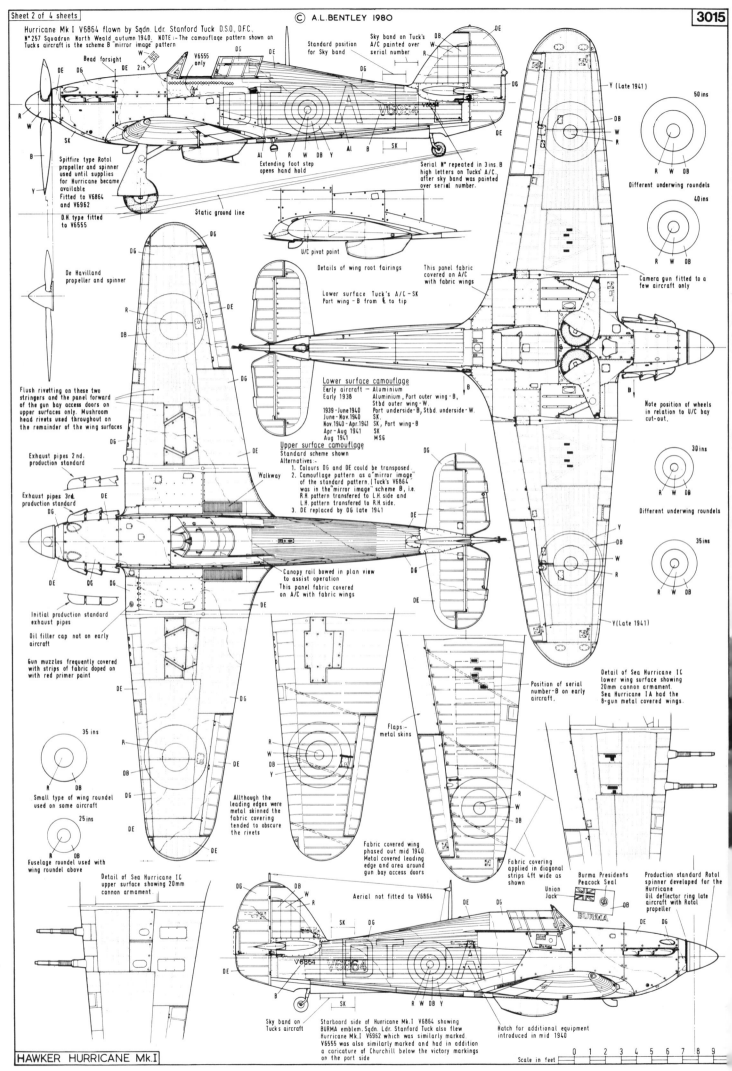

Bead forsight

DE   DG

W   T
2 in

V6555
only

Standard position
for Sky band

Sky band on Tuck's
A/C painted over
serial number

Y (Late 1941)

50 ins

Different underwing roundels

40 ins

R   W   DB

Spitfire type Rotol
propeller and spinner
used until supplies
for Hurricane became
available
Fitted to V6864
and V6962

Extending foot step
opens hand hold

Serial N° repeated in 3ins. B
high letters on Tucks' A/C.
after sky band was painted
over serial number.

D.H. type fitted
to V6555

Static ground line

U/C pivot point

Details of wing root fairings

Lower surface Tuck's A/C - SK
Port wing - B from ℄ to tip

This panel fabric
covered on A/C
with fabric wings

Camera gun fitted to a
few aircraft only

De Havilland
propeller and spinner

Lower surface camouflage
Early aircraft — Aluminium
Early 193B   Aluminium, Port outer wing - B,
                  Stbd outer wing - W.
1939 - June 1940 Port underside - B, Stbd. underside - W.
June - Nov. 1940 SK.
Nov. 1940 - Apr. 1941 SK, Port wing - B
Apr - Aug 1941   SK
Aug 1941   MSG

Flush rivetting on these two
stringers and the panel forward
of the gun bay access doors on
upper surfaces only. Mushroom
head rivets used throughout on
the remainder of the wing surfaces

Upper surface camouflage
Standard scheme shown
Alternatives :-
1. Colours DG and DE could be transposed.
2. Camouflage pattern as a "mirror image"
   of the standard pattern. (Tuck's V6864
   was in the "mirror image" scheme B. i.e.
   R.H. pattern transferred to L.H. side and
   L.H. pattern transferred to R.H. side.
3. DE replaced by OG late 1941

Note position of wheels
in relation to U/C bay
cut-out.

Exhaust pipes 2nd.
production standard

Walkway

Exhaust pipes 3rd.
production standard

Canopy rail bowed in plan view
to assist operation

This panel fabric covered
on A/C with fabric wings

30 ins

Different underwing roundels

35 ins

R   W   DB

Initial production standard
exhaust pipes

Oil filler cap not on early
aircraft

Gun muzzles frequently covered
with strips of fabric doped on
with red primer paint

Position of serial
number - B on early
aircraft.

Y (Late 1941)

Detail of Sea Hurricane IC
lower wing surface showing
20mm cannon armament.
Sea Hurricane IA had the
8-gun metal covered wings.

35 ins

Small type of wing roundel
used on some aircraft

25 ins

R   DB

Fuselage roundel used with
wing roundel above

Allthough the
leading edges were
metal skinned the
fabric covering
tended to obscure
the rivets

Flaps -
metal skins

Fabric covering
applied in diagonal
strips 4ft wide as
shown

Fabric covered wing
phased out mid 1940.
Metal covered leading
edge and area around
gun bay access doors

Burma Presidents
Peacock Seal

Union
Jack

BURMA

Production standard Rotol
spinner developed for the
Hurricane
Oil deflector ring late
aircraft with Rotol
propeller

Detail of Sea Hurricane IC
upper surface showing 20mm
cannon armament.

Aerial not fitted to V6864

V6864   V6864

Sky band on
Tucks aircraft

Starboard side of Hurricane Mk.I V6864 showing
BURMA emblem. Sqdn. Ldr. Stanford Tuck also flew
Hurricane Mk.I V6962 which was similarly marked.
V6555 was also similarly marked and had in addition
a caricature of Churchill below the victory markings
on the port side

Hatch for additional equipment
introduced in mid 1940

HAWKER HURRICANE Mk.I

Scale in feet   0 1 2 3 4 5 6 7 8 9

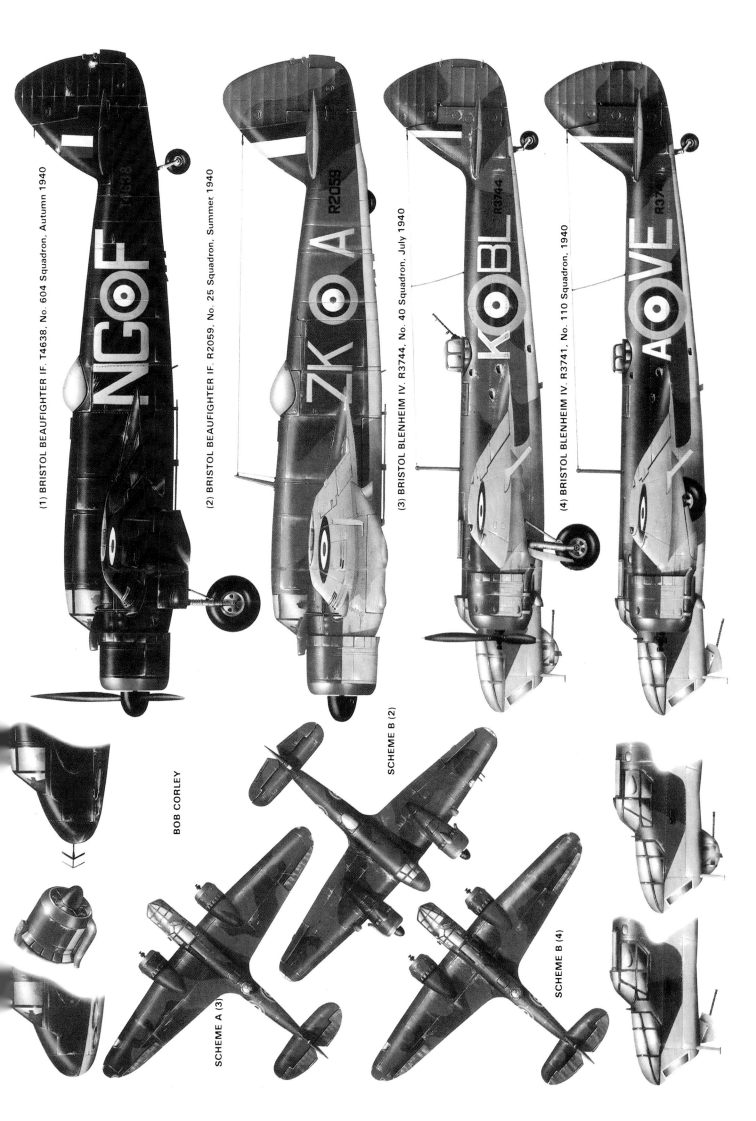

(1) BRISTOL BEAUFIGHTER IF. T4638, No. 604 Squadron, Autumn 1940

(2) BRISTOL BEAUFIGHTER IF. R2059, No. 25 Squadron, Summer 1940

(3) BRISTOL BLENHEIM IV. R3744, No. 40 Squadron, July 1940

(4) BRISTOL BLENHEIM IV. R3741, No. 110 Squadron, 1940

BOB CORLEY

SCHEME B (2)

SCHEME A (3)

SCHEME B (4)

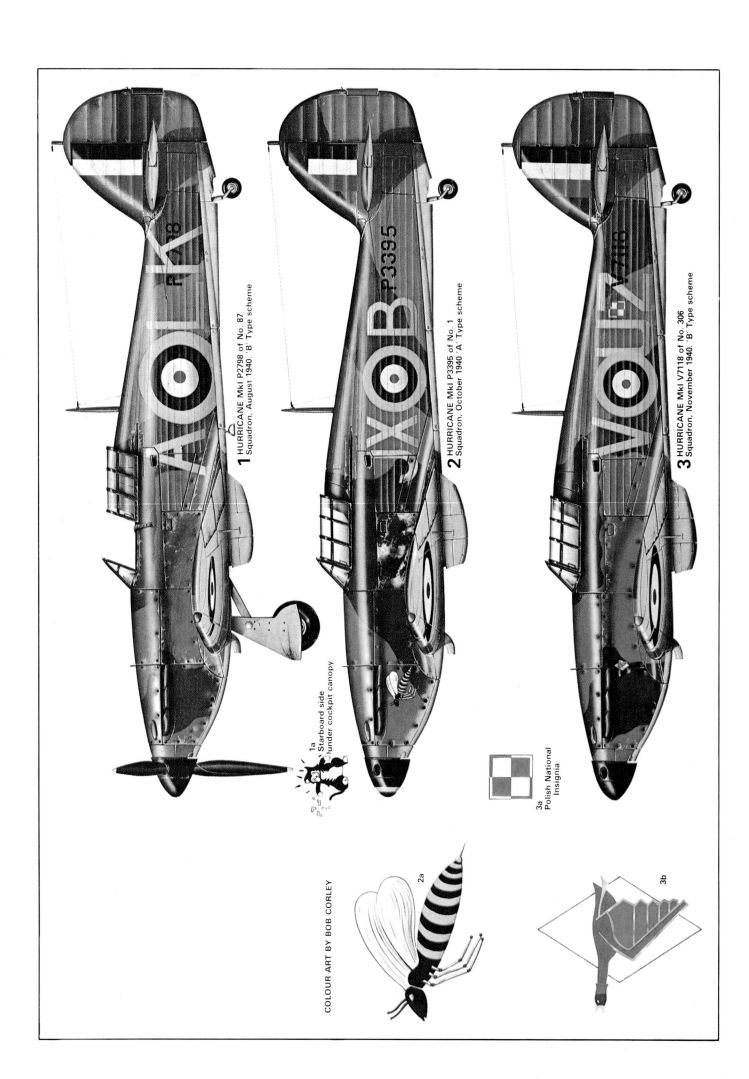

1 HURRICANE MkI P2798 of No. 87 Squadron. August 1940. 'B' Type scheme

1a Starboard side under cockpit canopy

2 HURRICANE MkI P3395 of No. 1 Squadron, October 1940 'A' Type scheme

2a

3 HURRICANE MkI V7118 of No. 306 Squadron. November 1940. 'B' Type scheme

3a Polish National Insignia

3b

COLOUR ART BY BOB CORLEY

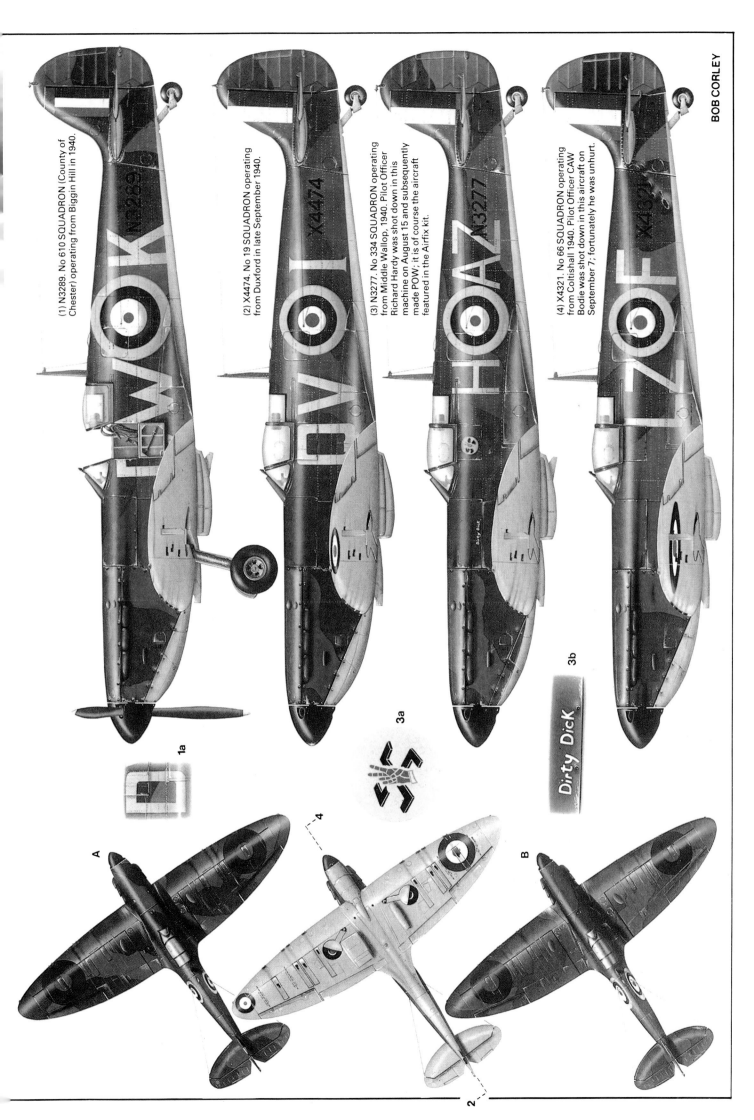

(1) N3289. No 610 SQUADRON (County of Chester) operating from Biggin Hill in 1940.

1a

(2) X4474. No 19 SQUADRON operating from Duxford in late September 1940.

(3) N3277. No 334 SQUADRON operating from Middle Wallop, 1940. Pilot Officer Richard Hardy was shot down in this machine on August 15 and subsequently made POW; it is of course the aircraft featured in the Airfix kit.

3a

3b

Dirty Dick

(4) X4321. No 66 SQUADRON operating from Coltishall 1940. Pilot Officer CAW Bodie was shot down in this aircraft on September 7; fortunately he was unhurt.

BOB CORLEY

A

B

4

2

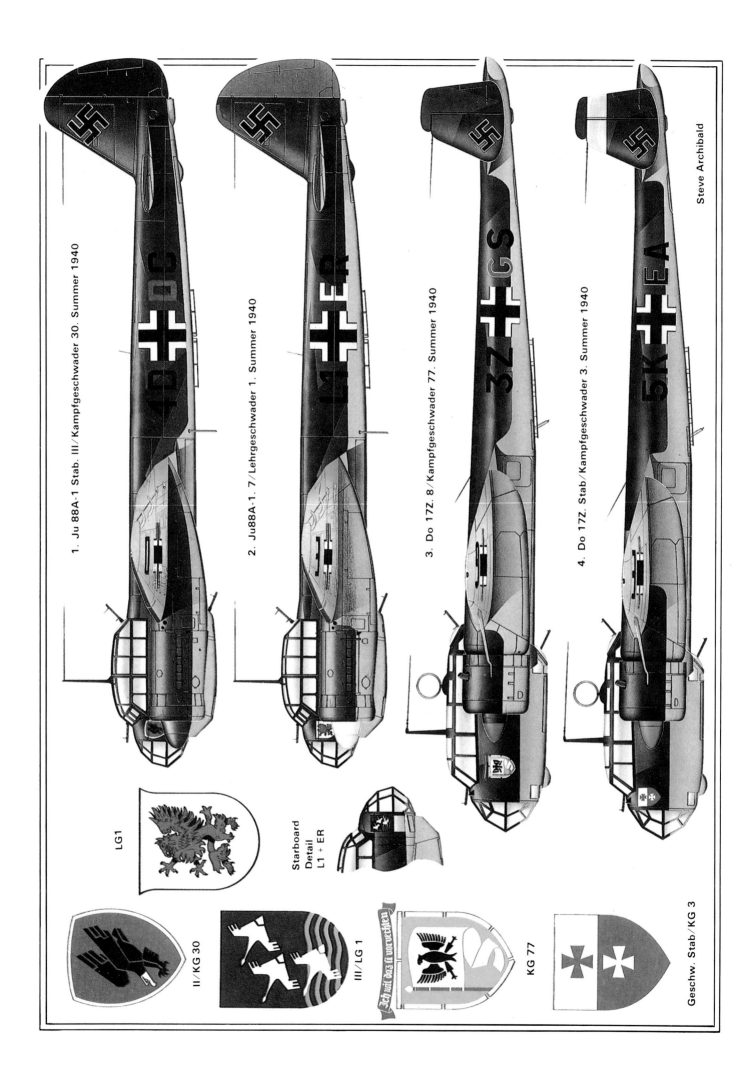

1. Ju 88A-1 Stab. III / Kampfgeschwader 30. Summer 1940

2. Ju88A-1. 7 / Lehrgeschwader 1. Summer 1940

3. Do 17Z. 8 / Kampfgeschwader 77. Summer 1940

4. Do 17Z. Stab / Kampfgeschwader 3. Summer 1940

Steve Archibald

LG1

Starboard
Detail
L1 + ER

II / KG 30

III / LG 1

KG 77

Geschw. Stab / KG 3

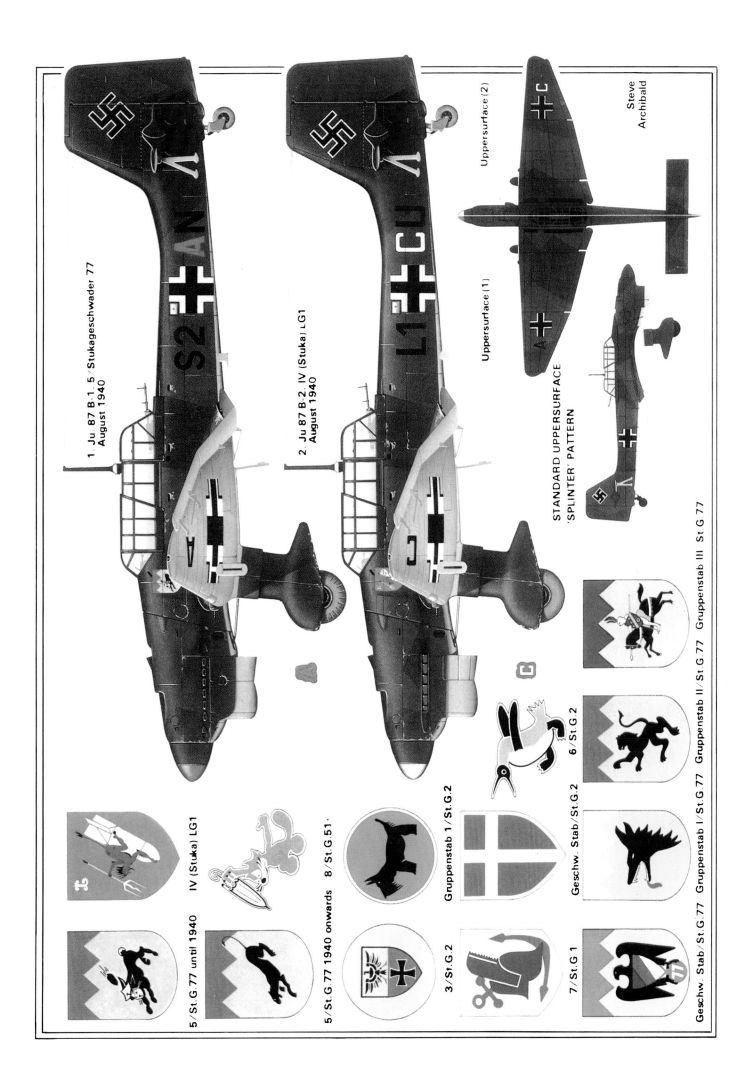

1. Ju. 87 B-1. 5 / Stukageschwader 77
August 1940

2. Ju 87 B-2. IV (Stuka) LG1
August 1940

Uppersurface (2)

Uppersurface (1)

STANDARD UPPERSURFACE
'SPLINTER' PATTERN

Steve
Archibald

IV (Stuka) LG1

5/St.G.77 until 1940

5/St.G.77 1940 onwards

8/St.G.51

Gruppenstab 1/St.G.2

3/St.G.2

6/St.G.2

Geschw. Stab/St.G.2

7/St.G.1

Geschw. Stab/St.G.77   Gruppenstab I/St.G.77   Gruppenstab II/St.G.77   Gruppenstab III St.G.77

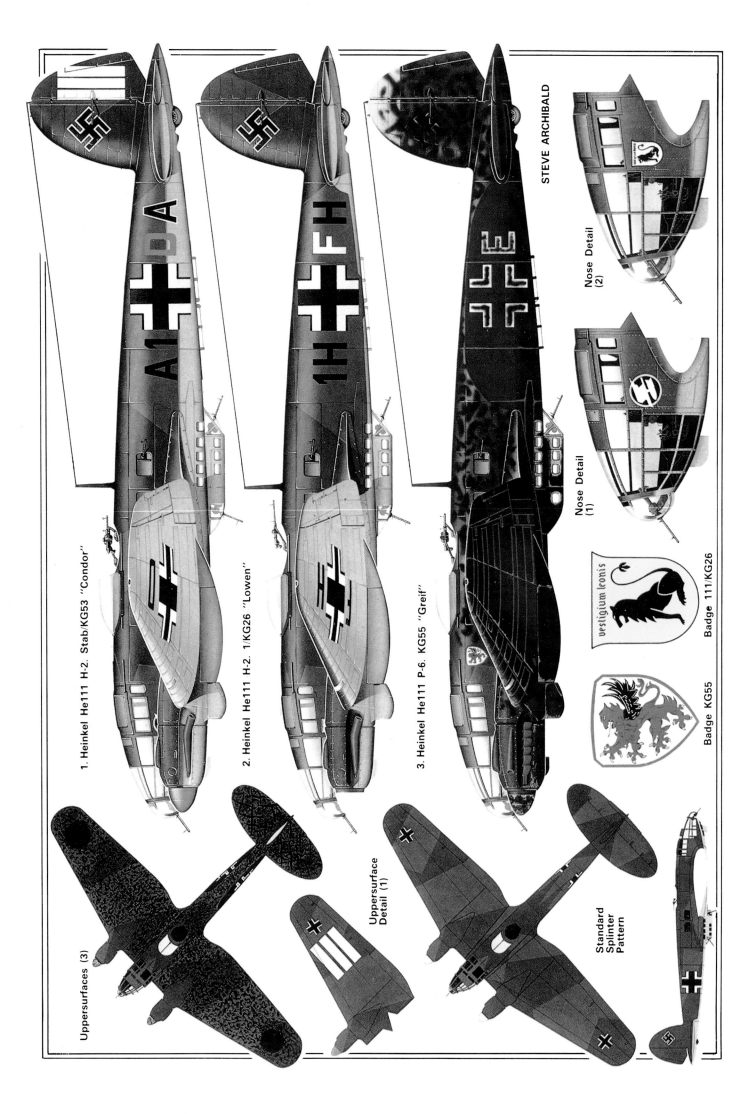

1. Heinkel He111 H-2. Stab/KG53 "Condor"

2. Heinkel He111 H-2. 1/KG26 "Lowen"

3. Heinkel He111 P-6. KG55 "Greif"

STEVE ARCHIBALD

Nose Detail
(2)

Nose Detail
(1)

vestigium leonis

Badge 111/KG26

Badge KG55

Uppersurfaces (3)

Uppersurface
Detail (1)

Standard
Splinter
Pattern

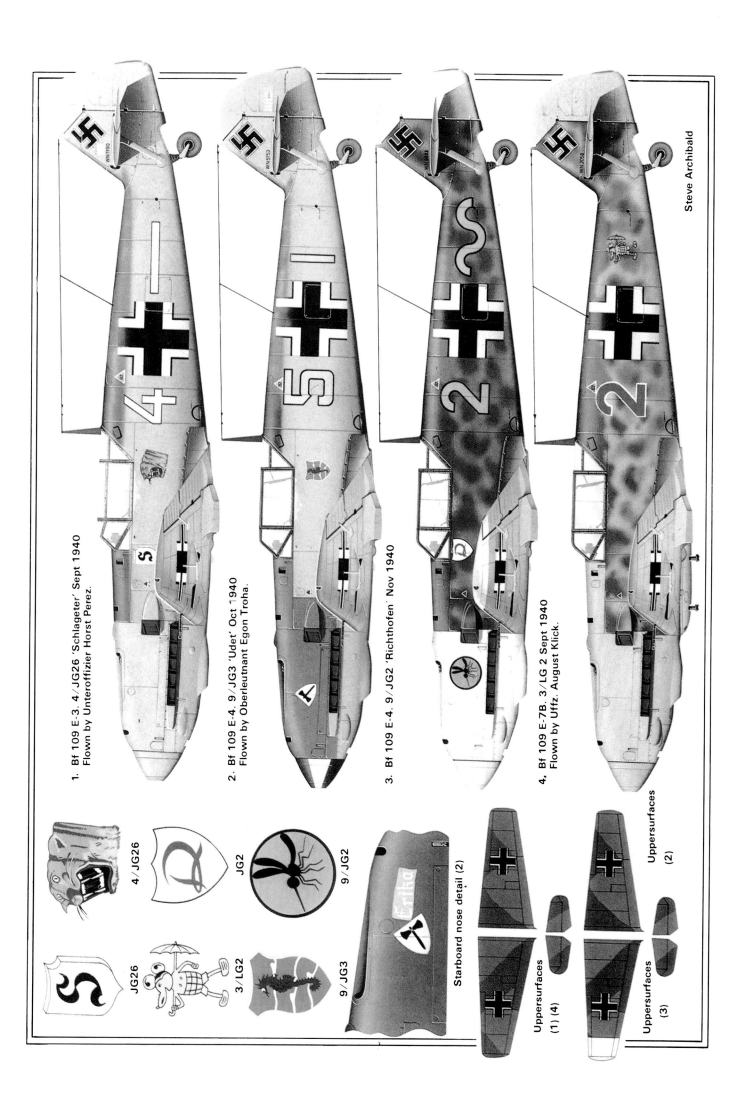

1. Bf 109 E-3. 4/JG26 'Schlageter' Sept 1940
Flown by Unteroffizier Horst Perez.

2. Bf 109 E-4. 9/JG3 'Udet' Oct 1940
Flown by Oberleutnant Egon Troha.

3. Bf 109 E-4. 9/JG2 'Richthofen' Nov 1940

4. Bf 109 E-7B. 3/LG 2 Sept 1940
Flown by Uffz. August Klick.

Steve Archibald

4/JG26

JG2

9/JG2

JG26

3/LG2

9/JG3

Starboard nose detail (2)

Uppersurfaces
(1) (4)

Uppersurfaces
(3)

Uppersurfaces
(2)

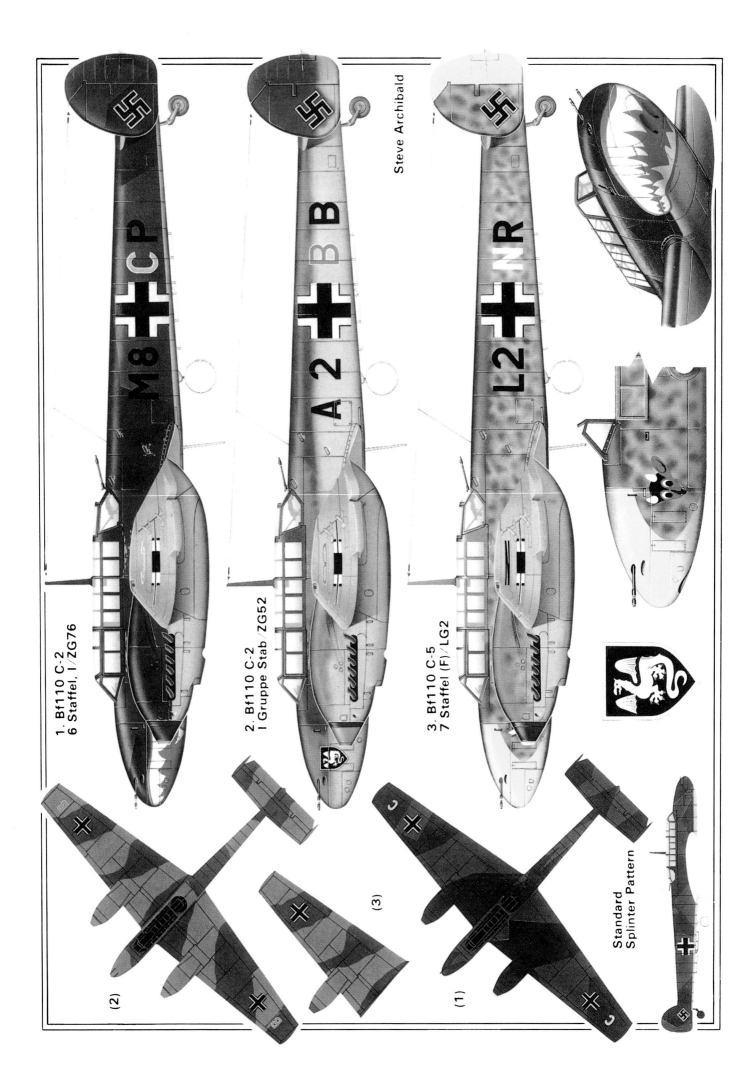

Steve Archibald

1. Bf110 C-2
6 Staffel, I /ZG76

2. Bf110 C-2
I Gruppe Stab/ZG52

3. Bf110 C-5
7 Staffel (F)/LG2

Standard
Splinter Pattern

© A.L.BENTLEY 1980

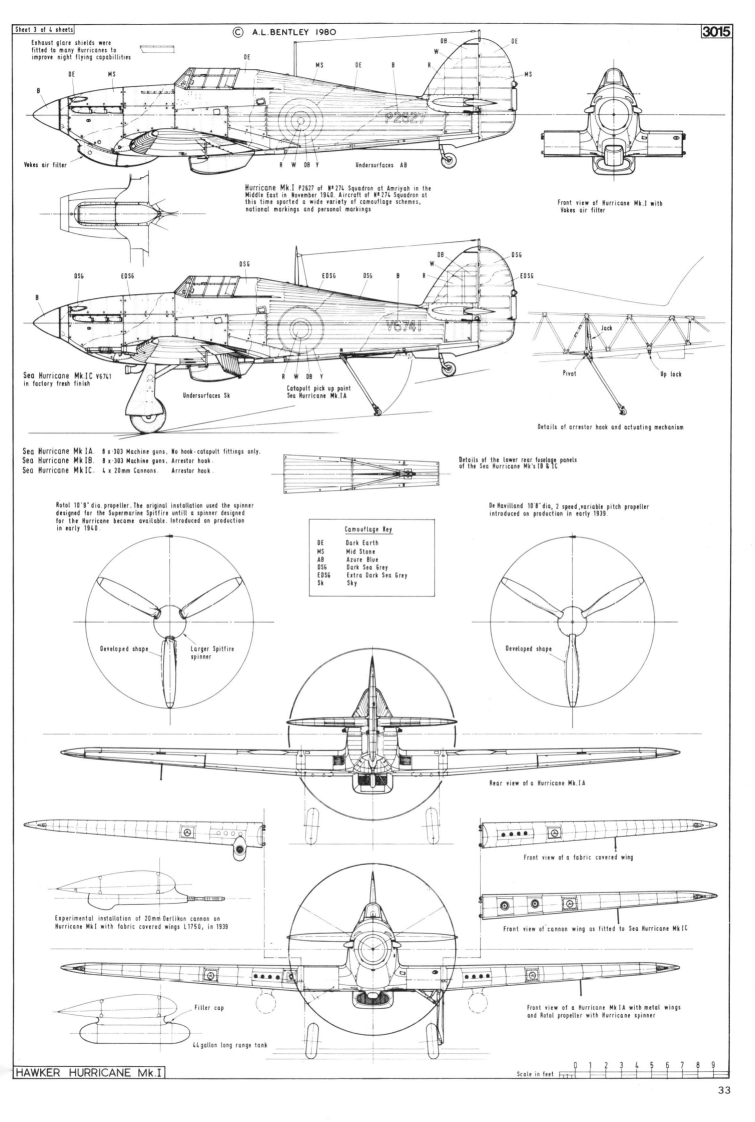

Exhaust glare shields were fitted to many Hurricanes to improve night flying capabillities

DE   MS

B

Vokes air filter

DE   MS   DE   B   DB   DE   W   R   MS

P2627

R   W   DB   Y   Undersurfaces AB

Hurricane Mk.I P2627 of Nº 274 Squadron at Amriyah in the Middle East in November 1940. Aircraft of Nº 274 Squadron at this time sported a wide variety of camouflage schemes, national markings and personal markings

Front view of Hurricane Mk.I with Vokes air filter

DSG   EDSG   EDSG   DSG   B   DB   DSG   W   R   EDSG

B

V6741

R   W   DB   Y   Undersurfaces Sk

Sea Hurricane Mk.IC V6741 in factory fresh finish

Catapult pick up point Sea Hurricane Mk.IA

Jack

Pivot   Up lock

Details of arrestor hook and actuating mechanism

Sea Hurricane Mk IA.   8 x ·303 Machine guns.   No hook - catapult fittings only.
Sea Hurricane Mk IB.   8 x ·303 Machine guns.   Arrestor hook.
Sea Hurricane Mk IC.   4 x 20mm Cannons.   Arrestor hook.

Details of the lower rear fuselage panels of the Sea Hurricane Mk's IB & IC

Rotol 10'9" dia. propeller. The original installation used the spinner designed for the Supermarine Spitfire untill a spinner designed for the Hurricane became available. Introduced on production in early 1940.

De Havilland 10'8" dia, 2 speed, variable pitch propeller introduced on production in early 1939.

Camouflage Key	
DE	Dark Earth
MS	Mid Stone
AB	Azure Blue
DSG	Dark Sea Grey
EDSG	Extra Dark Sea Grey
Sk	Sky

Developed shape   Larger Spitfire spinner

Developed shape

Rear view of a Hurricane Mk.IA

Front view of a fabric covered wing

Experimental installation of 20mm Oerlikon cannon on Hurricane MkI with fabric covered wings L1750, in 1939

Front view of cannon wing as fitted to Sea Hurricane MkIC

Filler cap

44 gallon long range tank

Front view of a Hurricane MkIA with metal wings and Rotol propeller with Hurricane spinner

HAWKER HURRICANE Mk.I

0 1 2 3 4 5 6 7 8 9
Scale in feet

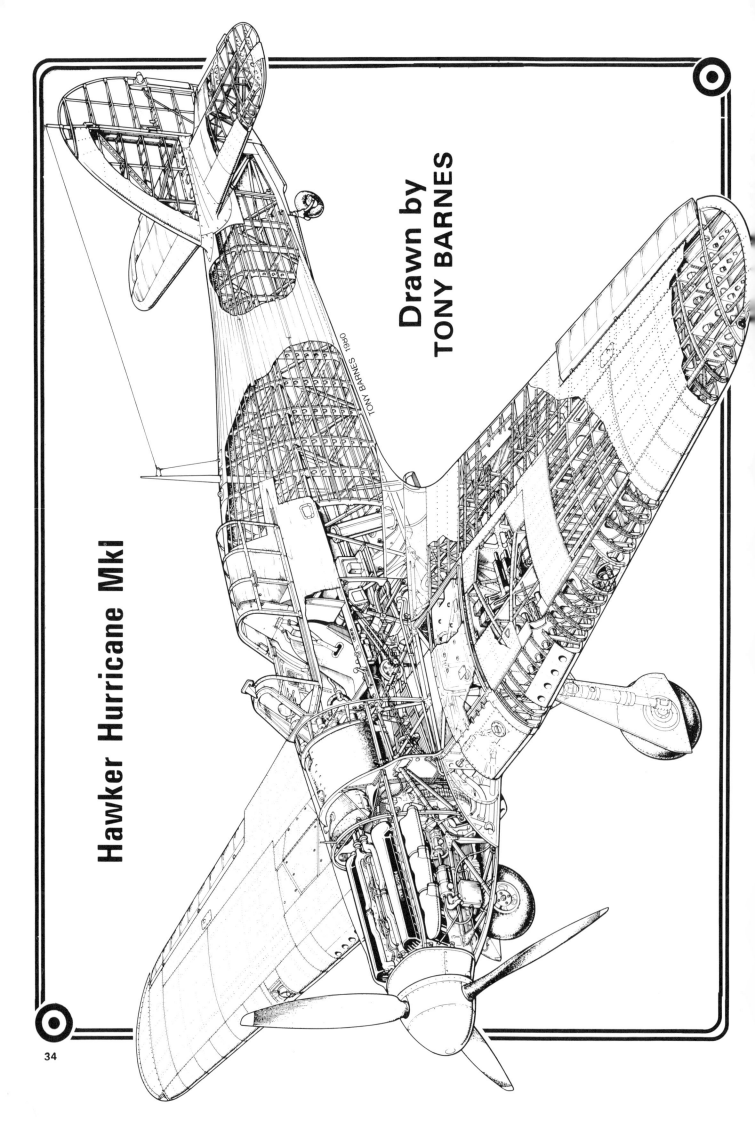

Hawker Hurricane MkI

Drawn by TONY BARNES

TONY BARNES 1980

Spitfire 1

Superdetailing the Airfix kit

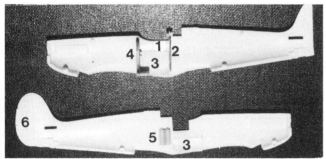

Author's model represents X4326 of No 66 Squadron as based at Kenley in September/October 1940. . . . Spitfire V cockpit (similar to Mk1) reveals Radio Contactor unit beneath rear windscreen frame and note rack and spare bulbs for the reflector sight. All consoles and instruments were normally painted black.

STAGE 1

The internal surfaces of both fuselage halves should be generally cleaned up, removing all moulded pegs and thinning out the cockpit sills especially. Cut away the port side entry door and fill the corresponding gap on the starboard half with plastic sheet (1). Add a rear bulkhead (2) and side panels (3), also from plastic sheet, an instrument panel from an old **Heller** Mk 1 (4), and oxygen bottles from sprue (5). Fuselage 'ribbing' can be simulated from small lengths of stretched sprue carefully affixed with liquid cement.

At this stage also reduce the heavy rib detail on the rudder and score and cut the trim tab (6) to a new position.

STAGE 2

The construction of the wing is explained fully in **Stage 5**, but here a floor from plastic sheet can be seen (1) and cutouts made by removal of the centre-section flaps (3). A new pilot's seat (2) is a modified Heller item suitably cut down and refined. Cockpit parts are the poorest area of Airfix's kit but as shown extra detail is fairly easily applied.

STAGE 3

Fit out cockpit areas referring to relevant source material. Most of the detail is fabricated from plastic sheet (3) and strip scrap (2).

and strip scrap (2). Elevator control horns and cables from sprue (1) are attached to starboard fuselage. Paint everything *Interior Green*, then drybrush in a lighter shade to obtain highlighted detail. Kit gunsight is modified, suitable decal dials found for the instrument panel and a new control column from sprue is added last of all.

STAGE 4

Having painted all internal areas, cement the fuselage halves together and tape whilst cement hardens. Note that the rudder has been cut and repositioned not forgetting to remove moulded actuating rod between fuselage and rudder horn (1). Refine lips of cockpit sills where the door will later be fitted (2).

STAGE 5

Before affixing to the fuselage, the wing parts come in for a certain amount of attention. First remove the moulded navigation lights, then centre-section flaps using a *sharp* craft knife. File away flaps moulded to upper wing halves (*parts 12 and 14*) cleaning up with Wet n'Dry paper.

Thin down leading and trailing edges at the same time reducing the thickness of panel lines before cementing wing assembly in place, and note that the correct dihedral may be lost if wing roots are not pared down a little beforehand. Tape is also stretched across the wing tips to hold the assembly at the correct angle, whilst glue sets (2). Reduce size of engine cowl fasteners (1) by sanding then clean up all joints and remove IFF lamp on upper fuselage spine and the lamp on the rudder.

STAGE 6

Other modifications to the wing include cutting out the slot for the flap actuating rod having already thinned down the areas beneath. Saw out aileron gaps (3) then cut the elevators away to re-cement at correct angle (2) not forgetting attention to the trim tabs.

STAGE 7

Add rib detail to flap area either by light scoring (1) or applying fine lengths of stretched sprue. Wheel wells should be improved by boxing in with 10 thou plastic sheet (2); later these insertions are trimmed flush with the wing and sanded smooth with any resultant gaps judiciously filled. Drill out all eight gun ports (3) and then fill the rather heavy panel lines around the nose area (4). Considerable filler may be required on the rear wing fuselage joint (5) and this is the last job before final sanding and cleaning prior to painting.

I do not intend to waste reader's time by describing the finish of the typical 1940 schemes as these are ably described by Neil Robinson and ably illustrated by Bob Corley. The model was painted in **Humbrol** Authentics with most of the insignia from **Letraset** M11, and M14 RAF sheets. **Modeldecal** sheet No. 33 yielded the serial block with **Microscale's** sheet 72-140 the stencil legends. Model painting was virtually completed before final assembly.

STAGE 8

A new entry door (1) is made from a curved piece of 10 thou plastic sheet scored and the outline thickness made from fine lines of PVA glue, and when painted adding the crowbar (from stretched red sprue) which is held in place with varnish. Before painting the airscrew, the blades (2) need attention from the modeller in order to reduce their rather heavy profiles.

STAGE 9

The separate flaps which will now hang from the wing are cut from 10 thou plastic sheet scored or sprue added on the inner surface to represent ribbing. Four separate pieces are required (1

and 5) and do not forget the flap actuating rods (sprue) and doors (5 thou plastic sheet) which are added after flaps have been painted and installed, (see sketch). Both undercarriage doors (2) will need their edges refined by careful sanding and 'flats' should be made on the 'tyres' before attaching to the wing. Final details include filling the cartridge ejection shutes with dark grey paint (3) and the signal lamp recess (4) with orange paint. Later fill with PVA glue or Microscale *Kristal Kleer*, gloss varnishing when dry.

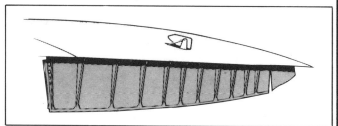

Now preserved at Hendon, Mk1 Spitfire reveals trim tab detail, fabric covered control surfaces, tail wheel and lamp housing styles. Above, the simplified approach to that flap actuating rod—sprue and scrap will suffice in 1/72nd.

Final Suggestions

Cockpit area can be completed by adding a Sutton Harness from draughting tape painted Khaki and cut into strips — but before attaching the canopy spray model overall with semi-matt clear varnish. Wing fuselage rudder lights are painted their appropriate colours of red, green and white then 'glazed' with a dab of Kristal Kleer. Our canopy was carefully razor sawn into three pieces, the edges refined and then glued to the model with careful application of PVA adhesive, the hood being in the slid back position. Finally the three aerial wires are added from sprue with slight dry brushing of Dark Earth around the wheels to complete the job.

REFERENCES WE CONSULTED
COCKPIT DETAIL

Pilot's Notes, Spitfire MkII. *From Air Data Publications, Back West Crescent, St Annes on Sea, Lancashire.* One of scores of official reproductions of original documents provide invaluable data and illustration to aid modellers on creating miniature cockpits.

Spitfire, Classic Aircraft No. 1 First in the series published by *Patrick Stephens Ltd* and written by Roy Cross and Gerald Scarborough to support the Airfix 1/24th Spitfire Mk1. A superb collection of references include colour schemes, detailed description of modelling the big kit, cockpit data (especially good) and of course several of the features discussed here, i.e. pilot's harness, flap details, undercarriage units etc. Reviewed SM *October 1972.*

GENERAL DRAWINGS

The best scale drawings available of the Mk1 include ASP Plan Pack 2896 (see page 606) from ASP Plans Service, (see also *SM October* 1969), and those by Alfred Grainger which appear in the excellent **Aerodata No. 2**, reviewed SM *June 1978.*

COLOURS

The best references include the **Ducimus Camouflage and Markings** No 1 written by *James Goulding,* which includes accurate camouflage patterns and superb colour illustrations. This publication was reviewed with some detail in SM *January* 1971. Alf Grainer's aforementioned Aerodata also provides some excellent colour, then there is **Aircam/Airwar 1 'RAF Fighter' units Europe 1939-42** by *Bryan Philpott* published by **Osprey,** (Reviewed SM *August* 1977).

Few will argue that the definitive book on the Battle itself is *Frank Mason's* **'Battle over Britain'** originally published by *McWhirter Twins,* a superbly researched tome which includes a myriad of detail, colour drawings, and scores of photos. The book was reviewed in SM *December* 1969. If you are going to embark on this series, make this volume your first purchase or borrow a copy from your local library.

COLOURS AND MARKINGS

SPITFIRE Mk.I's were finished in Dark Green and Dark Earth uppersurfaces, in one of two standard camouflage patterns, referred to as A and B schemes and shown on the colour page. Up until June 1940, the undersurfaces carried a high visibility recognition scheme of Night, port and White starboard, divided equally down the centre line, or, with the nose underside forward of the wing leading edge, fuselage underside aft of the wing trailing edge and the tailplanes and elevators finished in Aluminium paint.

Although underwing roundels were not carried during the use of this scheme, the Air Ministry had ordered that aircraft operating over France should have underwing roundels applied, at unit level, which resulted in the inevitable variations. A later amendment ordered a Yellow outer ring to be applied to the roundel under the port, (Night) wing, but to avoid balance problems it did not overlap the aileron and was generally terminated at the aileron hinge line.

Spinners were finished in Night, remaining in this colour until November 1940, and only on very rare occasions were Spitfires seen with spinners in other colours.

Upperwing roundels had been standardised at 56 inch diameter Type B by May/June 1940, but some early delivery machines may still have sported the smaller 40 inch diameter Type B size, previously altered from the original 56 inch diameter pre-war Type A1, with the Yellow outer ring painted out and the Red and Blue rings increased in width to cover the White. Fuselage roundels had gone through a series of changes, but by late April had been fixed at Type A, of either 25 inch diameter for in-service modified roundels, or 35 inch diameter for new production machines.

However, an Air Ministry signal sent on the 1st May, ordered that all fuselage roundels should be encircled with an outer ring of Yellow, making them into Type A1.

For the majority of in-service Spitfires, this increased the fuselage roundel to 35 inch diameter, (it previously being a 25 inch Type A), but on machines with 35 inch diameter Type A roundels it increased it up to 49 inch diameter, as seen on the well known photographs of several of No. 610 Squadron's Spitfires, taken in late May 1940. Production machines were delivered with 35 inch Type A1 fuselage roundels which had been fixed as the standard size. An anomaly, that occurred at this time, was the application of an oversize 7 inch Dull Red centre spot on the fuselage roundels of many of the new production Spitfires, which is usually attributed to a draughtsman's error on Supermarine's master markings drawings! Who ever *was* responsible for this intriguing anomaly, we are indebted to Dick Ward who foresaw the need of modellers wishing to model Spitfires so marked, by including separate 7 inch Dull Red centre spots on his Modeldecal Sheet No. 39. This, together with sheet numbers 40 and 42, covers ALL the national markings variations to be found on Spitfires, (plus many other aircraft types), prior to, and including the Battle of Britain period.

At the same time as the introduction of the Yellow fuselage roundel outer ring, fin stripes were also adopted. Officially these should have been composed of three 7 inch wide bands, extending the full height of the fin, but variations of 5 inch, 6 inch, and 8 inch wide strips did occur.

In early June 1940, the familiar Sky undersurface was introduced. There has been much interesting controversy over the exact shade of this colour, mainly stemming from the descriptions of it at the time of its introduction, e.g. Duck Egg Blue and Duck Egg Green etc., and it seems quite probable that on in-service aircraft, the shade *did* vary due to such reasons as slight mixing errors, supply shortage of the correct primary colours resulting in the use of local unauthorised alternatives, and even the influence of the Yellow Chromate or Cerrux Grey primer coats.

I think it can be safely said that Spitfires *were* seen in rich shades of light blue, paler and/or brighter greenish shades, or varying shades of the standard Sky colour, but factory fresh machines would almost certainly have been finished in the official, correct shade of Sky.

Underwing roundels were not carried during this period, (exceptions being the few aircraft operating over the French mainland), until August 1940 when Type A underwing roundels were re-introduced for general use. The official size of these roundels was 50 inch diameter, but on in-service Spitfires there was a wide variation of both roundel diameters and their positioning; approx. 25 inch diameter located near the extreme wing tip being quite a common variation.

Fin stripes were also standardised at this time, as three 8 inch wide bands extending 27 inches up the fin, but it was well towards the end of September before any quantity of new production machines had been delivered with these revised markings.

Serial numbers were invariably carried on the rear fuselage, in 8 inch high Night characters, although there were cases of the serials being of slightly differing sizes, and very occasionally even in Medium Sea Grey.

The original order stating that the Medium Sea Grey code letters were to be 48 inches high, was qualified by an amendment allowing smaller letters to be used if the available space was insufficient. Due to the slim fuselage of the Spitfire, 30 inch high code letters appear to have been popular, although the larger 48 inch size were adopted by some Squadrons. The shade of these Medium Sea Grey letters did tend to vary from a pale, almost off white colour, to quite a dark grey, but this was possibly the effect of insufficient mixing or stirring.

An interesting feature of the upper/under surface colour demarcation, was the extent of the depth of the uppersurface camouflage colours on the nose. This varied from terminating along the straight, cowling panel, join line, to a lower demarcation, which could be said to follow the curve of the nose underside. The undersurface colour(s) along the rear fuselage also showed minor variations, either terminating at the rudder hinge line, or extending onto the base of the rudder itself. The former appears to generally apply to earlier Spitfires, and the latter to later production machines, although examples of both the variations can be found throughout Spitfire production.

Another feature of Battle of Britain period Spitfires, is the almost universal fitting of the variable pitch, small pointed spinner, De Havilland airscrew. The few Spitfire Mk.II's to reach the Squadrons in the autumn of 1940, all appear to be fitted with the improved, constant speed Rotol propeller with its blunt spinner, but practically all the Mk.I's employed the De Havilland unit. ☐

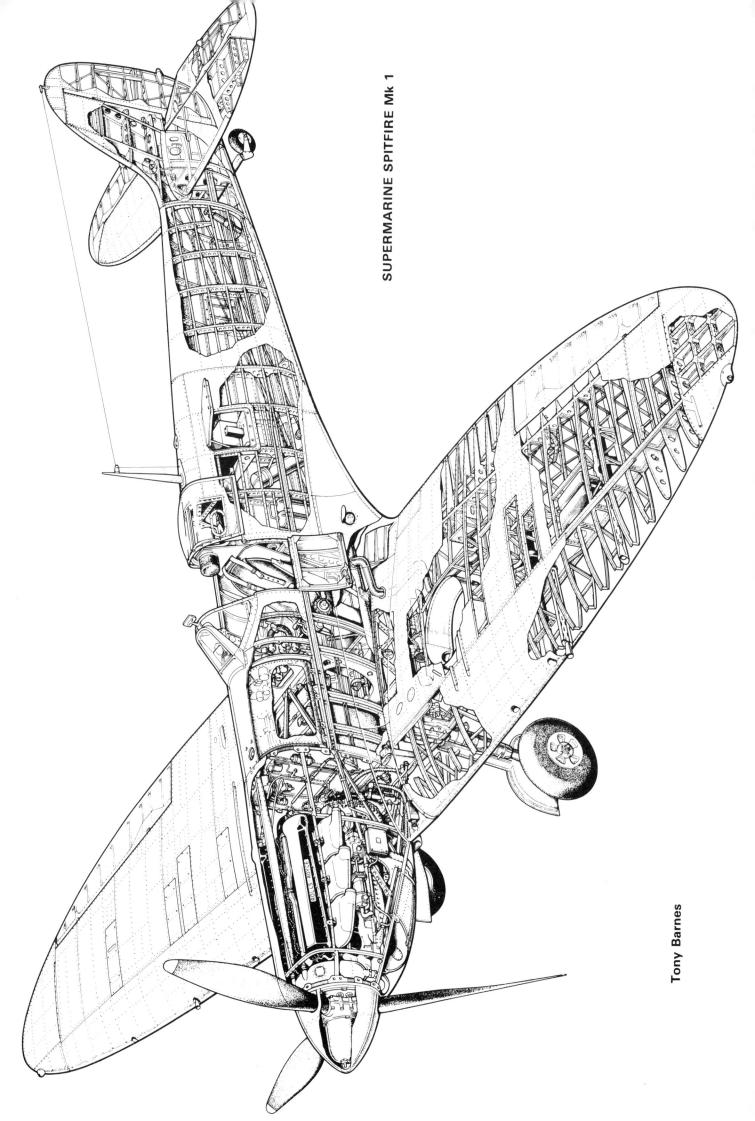

SUPERMARINE SPITFIRE Mk 1

Tony Barnes

Detail for the Scale Modeller
MARKINGS By P. G. COOKSLEY.

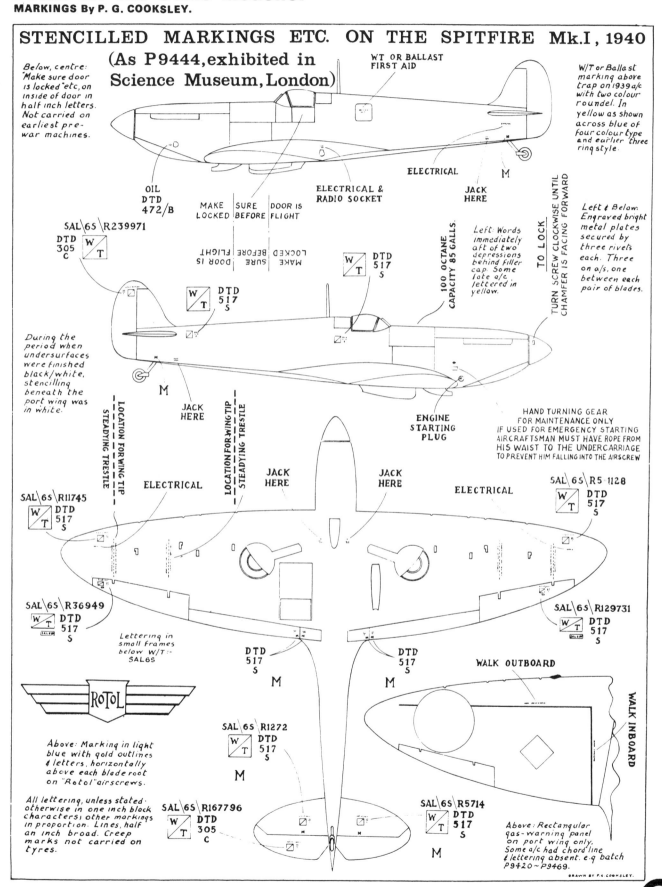

STENCILLED MARKINGS ETC. ON THE SPITFIRE Mk.I, 1940

(As P9444, exhibited in Science Museum, London)

Below, centre: Make sure door is locked etc, on inside of door in half inch letters. Not carried on earliest pre-war machines.

WT OR BALLAST FIRST AID

W/T or Ballast marking above trap on 1939 a/c with two colour roundel. In yellow as shown across blue of four colour type and earlier three ring style.

ELECTRICAL

JACK HERE

M

OIL DTD 472/B

MAKE LOCKED | SURE BEFORE | DOOR IS FLIGHT

ELECTRICAL & RADIO SOCKET

Left: Words immediately aft of two depressions behind filler cap. Some late a/c. lettered in yellow.

100 OCTANE CAPACITY 85 GALLS.

TO LOCK — TURN SCREW CLOCKWISE UNTIL CHAMFER IS FACING FORWARD

Left & Below: Engraved bright metal plates secured by three rivets each. Three on a/s, one between each pair of blades.

SAL\6S\R239971

DTD 305 C

W/T

DTD 517 S

W/T

DTD 517 S

During the period when undersurfaces were finished black/white, stencilling beneath the port wing was in white.

M

JACK HERE

LOCATION FOR WING TIP STEADYING TRESTLE

LOCATION FOR WING TIP STEADYING TRESTLE

JACK HERE

ENGINE STARTING PLUG

HAND TURNING GEAR FOR MAINTENANCE ONLY IF USED FOR EMERGENCY STARTING AIRCRAFTSMAN MUST HAVE ROPE FROM HIS WAIST TO THE UNDERCARRIAGE TO PREVENT HIM FALLING INTO THE AIRSCREW

SAL\6S\R11745

W/T DTD 517 S

ELECTRICAL

JACK HERE

JACK HERE

ELECTRICAL

SAL\6S\R5-1128

W/T DTD 517 S

SAL\6S\R36949

W/T DTD 517 S

Lettering in small frames below W/T:- SAL6S

DTD 517 S

M

DTD 517 S

M

WALK OUTBOARD

SAL\6S\R129731

W/T DTD 517 S

WALK INBOARD

Above: Marking in light blue with gold outlines & letters, horizontally above each blade root on "Rotol" airscrews.

All lettering, unless stated otherwise in one inch block characters; other markings in proportion. Lines, half an inch broad. Creep marks not carried on tyres.

SAL\6S\R1272

W/T DTD 517 S

M

SAL\6S\R167796

W/T DTD 305 C

SAL\6S\R5714

W/T DTD 517 S

Above: Rectangular gas-warning panel on port wing only. Some a/c had chord line & lettering absent. e.g batch P9420~P9469.

M

DRAWN BY P.G.COOKSLEY.

Part 2
Attackers

Do 17Z

Building the 'Blitzkrieg Bomber' in 1/72nd scale

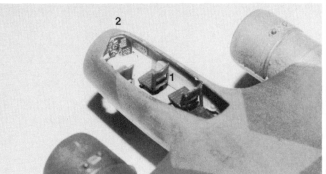

reproduced at the end of this feature. All paints were Humbrol *Authentics* mixed as appropriate.

Kit seats have been utilised (**1**) and a decal supplied by Frog makes a convincing instrument panel (**2**). Cockpit reference is minimal for this aircraft and I didn't really do the area justice on reflection — one reason for not sawing open any of the canopy windows! Interior is RLM 02 *Grau* with painted tape for seat harnesses etc. See accompanying drawings for details.

Assembly of the model is perfectly straightforward and basic assembly can be completed without the need to add internal detail first. The wing/fuselage joint (**1**) is poor thus requiring filler, and modifications can include chopping away ailerons (**2**) in order they may be re-sited later, and cleaning up the engine nacelles — especially the fronts and engine components — actually the cowling lips were later cut off my model to be replaced by **Monogram** items . . .

Undercarriage units (**1**) are modified by removing a small segment from each oleo and recementing thus giving the model a fully laden appearance. Wheels are replaced from more suitable items (**2**) — in this case from **Italaeri's** Ju 188 kit — and their bases heat flattened for appearance's sake. Some of the underfuselage nose transparencies, the flatter ones, are replaced from thinner plastic sheet (**3**). Interiors of wheel wells are also RLM 02 *Grau*.

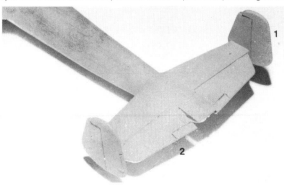

Remove both rudders (**1**) and after thinning down trailing edges re-attach at desired — but matching — attitudes: cut in gaps between trim tabs before cementing in place. Saw away elevators and drop accordingly (**2**) attending to trim tabs as before.

Stage 3

The camouflage pattern has already been applied in accordance with Steve Archibald's colour art and Neil Robinson's notes

The model represents 5K + EA of KG3 with its distinctive white formation markings on fin and starboard wing — see colour art. Markings were a mixture of those in the kit (mainly stencils) and **Letraset** Luftwaffe sheets M3, M4 and M6 with careful handpainting to achieve the yellow outlined letter E. Note here the colour demarcation lines (**1**) thinned down undercarriage doors (**2**), and reworked mudguards (**3**) which also required thinning down.

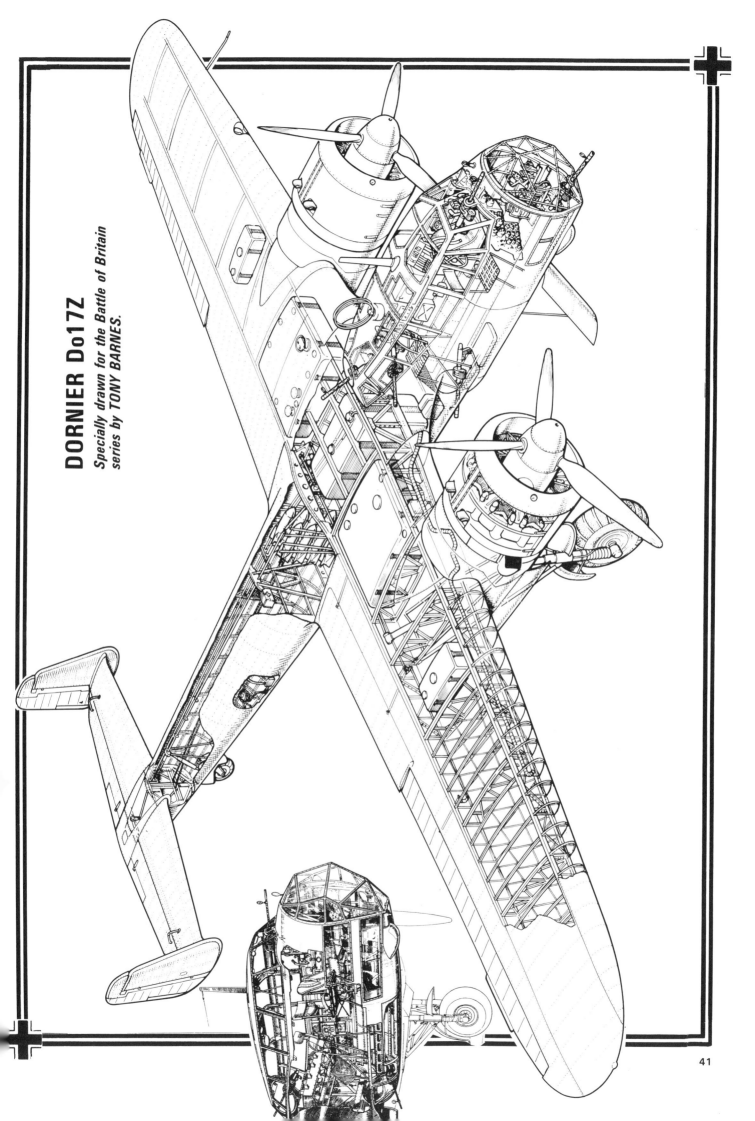

DORNIER Do17Z

Specially drawn for the Battle of Britain series by TONY BARNES.

41

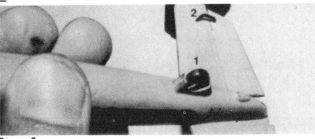

Stage 6

A small 'flat' has been filed on the integrally moulded tailwheel (**1**) and sprue actuating rods (**2**) replace the rather crude kit parts. The tailwheel demands careful painting, in common with most Luftwaffe aircraft the wheel hub itself is glossy black, the tyre a dark grey.

Stage 7

The general appearance of the kit transparencies is good and while the frames themselves are rather heavy they do facilitate painting. You trade a little accuracy for an easier life! The Monogram canopies won't fit anyway — I tried.

Guns (**1**) were replaced from spares box or built up from sprue and here it can be noted that the JG3 badge (**2**) has been repainted to create a more representative shape. Note stencil decals, walkways etc — all courtesy of the Frog decal sheet.

Stage 8

The model is completed with the addition of extra details. A new pitot (**1**) is made up from two differing diameter lengths of sprue. Wing tip lights (**2**) from coloured sprue and aerial cables from similar material (**3**). Note the white formation markings on fins and wing (**4**) created from segments of white **Scalemaster** decal film — Hannants of Lowestoft distribute.

REFERENCES WE CONSULTED

Cockpit Data

References for the Do 17Z are spartan to say the least and we are fortunate that Tony Barnes' has supplied a cutaway for this feature. Our other cockpit scrap view is another useful source for those wishing to super detail the rather cavernous interior of the Revell model.

GENERAL DRAWINGS AND COLOUR NOTES

I consulted three basic sources when modelling the Dornier, combining the best features of each to build up some kind of general picture of this elegant aircraft. *Profile No 164* — long out of print — *Aviation News* plans by Rainer Gliss and our own drawings available as Plan Pack 2895. For other colour schemes refer to the Karl Ries series (photos) and *Luftwaffe Camouflage and Markings* (Vol 2) by *JD Gallaspy and JR Smith* as reviewed in *SM* December 1977.

COLOURS AND MARKINGS

Camouflage followed the normal bomber practice of two tone green, *Schwarzgrun 70* and *Dunkelgrun 71,* uppersurfaces in a standard splinter pattern, with *Hellblau 65* undersides. The four digit identification code appeared on the fuselage sides, with two characters on either side of the fuselage cross. The *Geschwader* code, either a letter/number or number/letter combination, was positioned to the left of the cross, whilst to the right of the cross was the individual aircraft letter and *staffel* code letter. Identification codes were invariably painted in black with the exception of the individual aircraft letter which was normally painted in the *staffel* colour, or at least outlined in it. Certain other sub-types of the Do 17Z, such as the Do 17P and Do 215, which were also active during the Battle of Britain in the reconnaissance role, occasionally featured an anomaly peculiar to some *Aufklarungsgruppen* (reconnaissance wings), in that the individual aircraft letter instead of being painted in or outlined in the relevant *staffel* colour, was simply painted in black like the rest. Although this peculiarity was generally associated with reconnaissance aircraft, examples of bombers with all black fuselage codes are not unknown. (See "Luftwaffe Structure and Markings 1940" article in the *April 1980* issue of SM for further information). Individual aircraft letters were usually repeated under the wing tips, just outboard of the crosses, almost always in black, but no doubt exceptions did occur — as if just to prove the rule. Also, quite frequently, the individual aircraft letter, mainly in the *staffel* colour, was marked on the uppersurface of the wing tips, again just outboard of the crosses. Certain aircraft were recorded carrying temporary white formation aid symbols on the uppersurface of one, or more rarely, both wings, which usually took the form of an oblong bar or a stripe extending the full chord of the wing.

The upper/under surface camouflage demarcation line, especially noticeable on the engine nacelles, but apparent on the fuselage sides too, was open to some variation, and was possibly the result of machines being delivered from different factories. However care should be taken when painting a model of a Do 17Z, that the demarcation lines are correct for that particular machine.

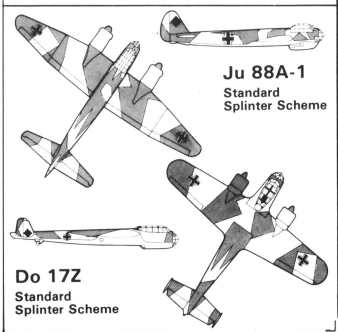

Ju 88A-1
Standard Splinter Scheme

Do 17Z
Standard Splinter Scheme

Heinkel He111P-6

Modifying and detailing the 1/72nd scale Italaeri kit

STAGE 1

Overall the assembly of Italaerei's kit is not terribly difficult thanks to a set of above average instructions and the general high standard of moulding. Nevertheless some problems were encountered when it came to fitting certain major components and we will be dealing with these a little later on.

Commence with the careful installation of fuselage and ventral gondola transparencies and adding the basic cockpit detail as supplied by the manufacturer. Fit an additional bulkhead and a floor (1) to fuselage interior cutting a slot in the latter to clear the ventral gondola position. The decision to install a great deal of internal detail amidships should be made at this stage with reference to our sketches and/or the full blown cutaways found on pages 126/127 and 129 of William Green's 'Wings of the Luftwaffe' – see references.

As little is seen through the upper gun position anyway, interior detail on the subject model was kept to a minimum applying only cursory additions before adding a coat of RLM Grau. The wings can be assembled next and the wheel wells (2) boxed in with 10 thou plastic card if desired.

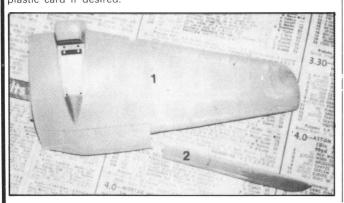

STAGE 2

Wings can be improved by reducing the thickness of the raised panel line detail with gentle sanding using wet n'dry paper (1). Ailerons should be removed (2) by gentle scoring with a sharp knife and cleaning up the edges with a file, later adding horns from scrap plastic and filing corresponding slots in the wing. Note that the chord of the undersurface is wider as it is for the flaps. The removal and depressed positioning for the latter is possible but some careful surgery will be required and this should be done prior to assembling wings; plastic card and filler being required to pack out the front face of each flap. A small fault with the kit lies in the actual flap contours. Viewed from directly behind the concave appearance is insufficient and the kit part will require bending/reshaping for absolute accuracy. Best to do this after they have been removed of course and preferably before the wings are cemented together. Photo below shows (or so we hope) the point under discussion.

STAGE 3

Fit of the main wings to the fuselage leaves something to be desired – at least it did on our model for the wing roots are simply not as deep as the corresponding fuselage roots resulting in an ugly step. The remedy is to deepen them by packing out with scrap plastic or wood, checking constantly until the correct depth is obtained and the parts lie flush. (Fig B) Once satisfied the wings can be carefully glued checking correct dihedral against scale drawings then all joints filled and smoothed (1). At this stage all other joint lines can be generally attended to (2).

STAGE 4

On the He IIIP version the airscoop on the engine nacelles appears on the port sides not starboard as the kit has them. It is not too difficult to knife the moulded scoops off (1) clean up their edges, reshape and recement on the opposite side. The resultant gap left by their removal (2) is plugged with a piece of plastic sheet,

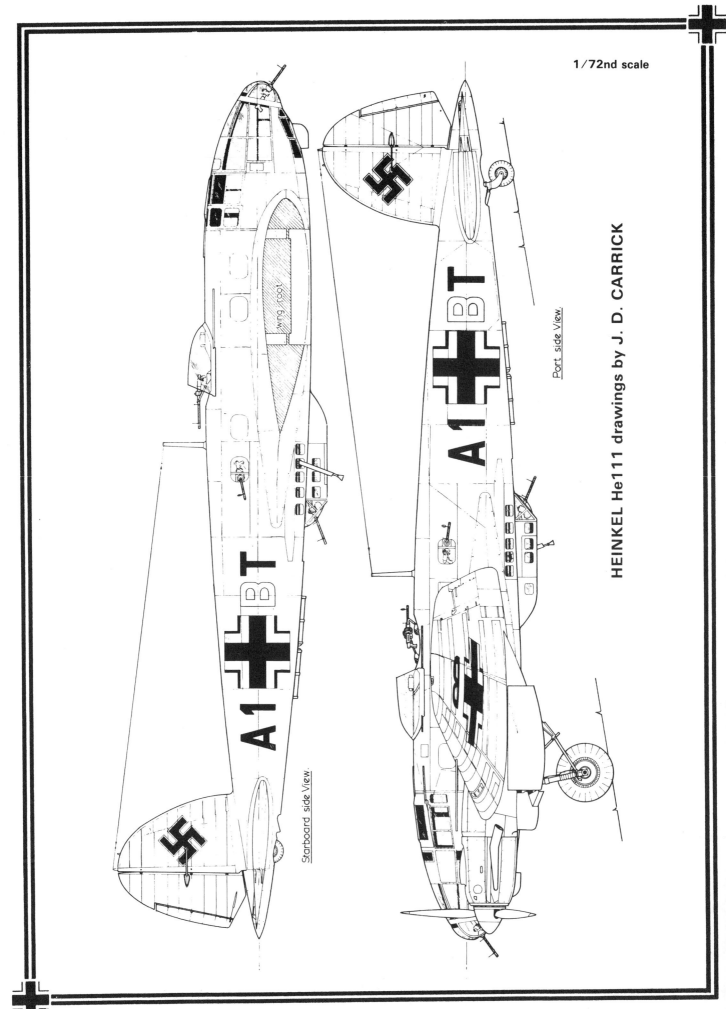

1/72nd scale

HEINKEL He111 drawings by J. D. CARRICK

Port side View.

Starboard side View.

wing root

the rear part of the nacelle moulded with the wing knifed away flush and the whole assembly smoothed over. See also sketch below.

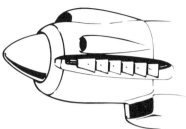

STAGE 5

Tailplanes feature separate elevators and thus provide the modeller the opportunity to cement these at a chosen angle, usually drooped on a parked aircraft (1). The separate rudder can also be angled (2) as can the servo tabs (3) all of which take much of the static appearance away from the completed model. Rivet detail on the tailplane is a little overscale and the lines of heads decidedly shaky; I preferred to sand them all off anyway. Finally when fitting tailplanes ensure that they line up square with the fin and mainplanes, some widening of the locating slots possibly being called for.

STAGE 6

On most of the Battle of Britain period Heinkel photographs, the forward two pairs of fuselage windows do not appear and as our chosen subject met these conditions, they were filled with Polyfilla (1). Exhaust stubs were modified (2) by reducing the length of the first stubs and smoothing round in order to accommodate breather pipes later (Nacelle shown tacked into place).

STAGE 7

The ventral gondola needs modification for the chosen version, the front position being solid – not glazed (**Fig A**). This easy modification is effected by filing off all frame lines of *part 48* and filling in the gun position. Later the trailing aerial fairlead made from scrap sprue is inserted through the second window of the port upper row – this needs predrilling of course and the sprue fairlead installed only after basic painting of the model has been completed.

1/72nd scale

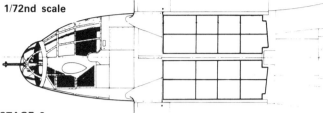

STAGE 8

Scribe in the bomb door positions underneath the fuselage using a straight edge and a metal pointer by transferring the shapes from the 1/72nd scale drawing (above) marking with a pencil before making the light scorings. Later clean up with wet n'dry paper. External racks, bombs, etc, are not required for this model and one is advised to save them as they may be useful for subsequent models to be discussed in this series.

STAGE 9

Cockpit detail as provided by Italaerei is fair but can obviously be added to especially if the upper canopy sliding hood is sawn away and modelled in the open position. I confined myself to adding an arm rest for the seat, harnesses, decal instrument dials on the port fuselage side, throttle console from sprue and scrap, plus boxing in of the floor beneath the pilot position and adding a support brace to the bomb aimer's 'couch'. A small instrument panel containing three dials is also added to the rear of the upper gun position referring again to our sketch page and **Fig B**.

File a small cutout on each wing tip for the navigation lights and install the modified exhausts. Breather pipes are added to the front stub by two lengths of thick sprue cemented to form a double tube then cut into four ⅛" lengths. These are then attached with liquid cement (**Fig B**).

Painting

I followed Steve Archibald's colour art to finish the model as an example of a He III P-6 of *Kampfgeschwader 55* in black night finish. The black applied to these Heinkels was a washable distemper which the ground crew roughly applied in the field. The distemper obliterated most of the national markings, the white areas of the fuselage cross being daubed over heavily and the best course is to follow the example set by full size practice, paint and finish the model, adding decals, varnish, etc, and apply the black, in our case Acrylic water colour, as the last stage. The three basic colours, *Greens 70/71* and *Hellblau 65* were mixed in accordance with Neil Robinson's text that follows these stages. The *entire* undersurfaces were painted Hellblau despite the fact that these will be painted over later.

Most WW2 Luftwaffe finishes imparted a dull sheen overall and this is fairly easy to simulate. A stiff nylon brush is loaded with

Heinkel Model Modifications

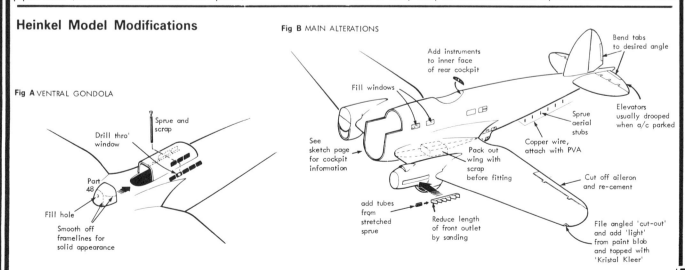

Fig B MAIN ALTERATIONS

Fig A VENTRAL GONDOLA

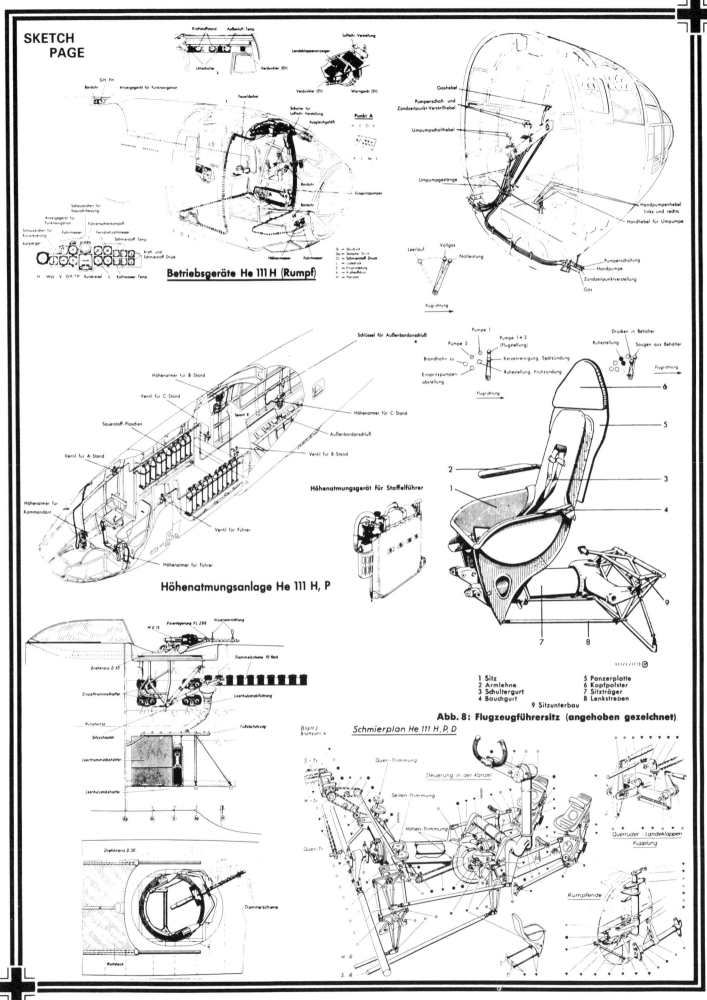

Betriebsgeräte He 111 H (Rumpf)

Höhenatmungsanlage He 111 H, P

Höhenatmungsgerät für Staffelführer

1 Sitz
2 Armlehne
3 Schultergurt
4 Bauchgurt
5 Panzerplatte
6 Kopfpolster
7 Sitzträger
8 Lenkstreben
9 Sitzunterbau

Abb. 8: Flugzeugführersitz (angehoben gezeichnet)

Schmierplan He 111 H, P, D

graphite dust (pencil lead shavings) and rubbed (buffed) over the model. This imparts a fair sheen, looks like worn metal over sharply defined edges and dulls down the basic colours most realistically, but do this *after* all decals have been applied in order to retain an overall uniformity. The KG55 badge was a compromise, since none of my spare decal sheets yielded the correct motif. **Microscale** sheet 72-16 contains a pair of shields for '4(H)/21 Bf109' and these were carefully retouched to closely match the style shown on Steve's colour plate. A quick spray over with semi-matt clear varnish (don't forget to mask those canopies first!) completes the job.

The black distemper is simulated by Acrylics mixed to a very dark grey and applied to the surfaces with a wide brush. Do not attempt to *totally* obliterate the Hellblau as the finish wore off quite considerably around leading edges, hatches, windows, etc, and when almost dry a pleasing effect can be obtained by rubbing a damp piece of cloth chordwise from the wing leading edges to stimulate wear. (See colour plates and model photos.)

Upper camouflage 'squiggles' were handpainted all over the majority of the upper surfaces and over national markings. The Acrylic paint will dry matt in contrast to the sheen of the basic finish, a distinction that tends to equate with the original rather nicely.

STAGE 10
Final details include the undercarriage assemblies which are superbly moulded by Italaerei and require little modification. The legs are dull metal with dark grey rubber gaiters and likely improvements include drilling out the axle centres and adding sprue brake cables.

Main and tail wheels need flattening by carefully heating the completed components and gently pressing onto a flat hard surface; the result should be a nicely 'belled out' type which looks far more in keeping with a heavily loaded bomber.

Add spots of colour for the navigation lights, topping with a blob of *Kristal Kleer* and a coat of gloss varnish, then add the Lorenz aerial stubs (sprue) and the aerial itself from copper wire. **(Fig B)**. Machine guns as supplied are excellent and can be improved by adding sights if desired from rings of fine wire and drybrushing with graphite dust. Spent cartridge collector bags can be made for the nose and upper guns where visible from old 1/72nd WW1 engine cylinders bent and it carefully painted to neatly represent the ribbed pouches of the original.

Finally attach the nose transparency with PVA glue, touch up paint where necessary and add the main aerial from dark grey stretched sprue.

REFERENCES WE CONSULTED
COCKPIT DETAIL
Wings of the Luftwaffe by William Green. Published by *Macdonald and Janes* this superlative book describes how captured enemy aircraft handled. Included are many superb cutaways of cockpits and structure, the He III is one of the best and there are scores of photographs.

GENERAL DRAWINGS AND MODELLING NOTES
The only set of scale drawings available so far is Plan Pack 2926 from ASP Plans Services (See also *SM September 1971* which is presented in two scales.

SCALE MODELS May 1977 *Ian Huntley's* article on improving the **Frog** Heinkel offered much useful information for super-detailing

and included additional colour plates in a double page spread.
PAM NEWS No. 17 Super builder's report on the Italaerei kit by the admirable and meticulous *E Lerwick Shaddon*. Innumerable hints, tips and suggestions for improvements will aid all builders of this fine kit and cannot be recommended highly enough.
SCALE MODELS March 1976 Again *Ian Huntley* helps Heinkel modellers with a discourse on Luftwaffe finishes with useful data Heinkel undercarriage finishes in particular.
MODELL MAGAZINE June 1977. *Heinz Mankau* describes modifications to the Italaerei kit in detail plus explains the modification for the P version types and discusses application of other additions.
COLOURS
The best references include the series of Karl Ries books (for photos) and **Luftwaffe Camouflage and Markings 1935-1945** (Vol 2) by *J R Smith* and *J D Gallaspy*, published by *Kookaburra* and reviewed in SM *December 1976*. Also recommended is Squadron Signal Publication's **He III in Action** by *Uwe Feist* and *Mike Dario* which includes plenty of good photos and in particular our KG 55 subject on page 26. But if you are *really* stuck for a subject refer to the colour drawings provided here after reading the final part of this feature – over to Neil Robinson. . .

COLOURS AND MARKINGS

THE largest of the twin engined aircraft operated by the *Kampfgeschwadern* during the Battle of Britain and like all contemporary Luftwaffe bombers of the periods, the He III was finished in one, (of at least two), uppersurface splinter pattern schemes, consisting of Schwarzgrun 70 (**Humbrol** HG15 RFC Green plus a dash of HB1 Dark Green and HU2 Olive Drab 41) and Dunkelgrun 71 (Humbrol HG2 Dunkelgrun 71 plus a dash of HB8 Dark Slate Grey), with Hellblau 65 (5 parts Humbrol HG3 Hellgrau 76 plus 2 parts MC12 Prussian Dragoon Blue) undersurfaces. *Balkenkreuze* (crosses) were positioned in the usual six positions, although the *Hakenkreuze* (swastikas) were either located fully on the fin, or slightly overlapping the fin and rudder hinge line. The four digit identification code appeared on the fuselage sides, the first two digits in black denoting the *Geschwader*, the third digit being the individual aircraft letter, either completely painted in, or simply outlined in, the staffel colour, and the fourth digit, in black, denoting the staffel within the *Geschwader* itself. Occasionally the full code was repeated under the wings in black, but the individual aircraft letter, also generally in black, positioned outboard of the underwing *Balkenkreuze* was becoming a more frequent practice by this time. Examples of the individual aircraft letter repeated on the extreme tips of the wing uppersurfaces was also not uncommon, and presumably as an aid to easier formation assembly, the summer of 1940 seeing the first attempts at really large daylight formations by any airforce, certain aircraft were recorded with large white oblong bars on one or both of the wing uppersurfaces, either side of the rudder, or even with the rudder completely overpainted in yellow.

With the introduction of night operations on a large and prolonged scale, many He III's were liberally daubed with temporary black undersurfaces, which extended onto the fuselage sides in some cases and even onto the uppersurfaces in the form of a mottle, often obliterating the white areas of the national insignia and the lighter colours used for the individual aircraft letters, as seen on the subject model. Propeller spinners were the usual areas for applying the *Staffel* or *Gruppe* colours, and the *Geschwader*, *Gruppe* or *Staffel* badges were invariably located on the forward fuselage immediatley behind the nose glazing.

Ju 87 Stuka

**Superdetailing the
Airfix Series 3
1/72nd scale kit**

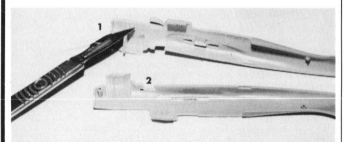

Stage 1

Excellent though the Airfix kit is, I still found it required a great deal of added detail before I was satisfied with the end result, although this should *not* be taken as a criticism of Airfix toolmakers. For reference it was very useful to have access to the large scale 1/24th version of the Stuka when it came to modifications with one area in particular — the bomb viewing window under the fuselage. Start by thinning down the lips of the nose radiator intake (**1**) using a sharp craft knife, cleaning up later with fine 'wet and dry'. Also cut out the aperture for that bomb viewing window (**2**) noting that the fore and aft edges should slope rearwards.

Stage 2

Thin out the rear flap area of the chin intake and add a plastic card blank (**1**) — cut to match the kit grille — and cement in place. Detail the cockpit insides with plastic card (**2**) and stretched sprue (**3**) before any painting is contemplated. I used MEK to attach all of these details.

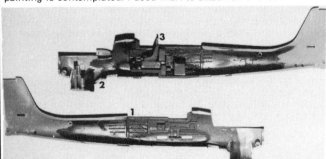

Author's completed model of the Junkers Ju 87 B-1 Stuka which has been modified and detailed to present a more realistic replica. Full details of the required changes are explained in the text.

Stage 3

The interior side detailing once completed is further enhanced by addition of the extras supplied with the kit. (**2**) Paint the interior surfaces of the shells in **Humbrol** *02 Grau* later dry-brushing in a lighter shade to accentuate all the detail, not forgetting to paint the inner surface of the intake flap (**2**). Extra consoles were added to the kit cockpit components and the seat filed to a more accurate and finer appearance (**3**).

Stage 4

Once the fuselage halves have been joined and cleaned up the wings and tail parts can be attached. Note the solid landing lap aperture (**1**) has been cut out, ailerons re-sited (**2**) the rudder cut off and re-angled (**3**) and the elevators drooped (**4**). The asymmetric scoop on the upper nose panel should be reamed out and a grille added from scored plastic card.

Stage 5

Dive brakes as moulded are overthick and can be improved by reducing their heavy appearance by filing and paring the edges with a craft knife (**1**). Airfix have seen fit to simplify the area behind the nose intake and the stepped portion of the forward fuselage (**2**) should be filled with scrap and a semi-circular front added which fits inside the flap. Later slots are cut into the nose assembly for the bomb cradle. The window (**3**) has been made up of four pieces of plastic card to form an internal box and is topped with a square of clear sheet. Have a look at a 1/24th scale kit to realise these shapes.

Stage 6

Slots for the bomb cradle have been cleaned up and any gaps in the modified 'nose' area filled before painting (1). Note that the tailwheel has been turned for added interest (2) and that the struts supporting the tailplanes are a little heavy and will require cleaning up prior to fitting in place. Bombs as supplied will also require refinement (3), the fins in particular will benefit from thinning or complete replacement with plastic card if you wish to go this far.

Stage 7

Once the painting is more or less complete (see Steve Archibald's artwork and Neil Robinson's notes for patterns and mixes), careful attention should be paid to details. Bombs can be painted Hellblau but note the rear casings supporting the fins are yellow. After applying the decals, touch in the dive brake as shown (1). Note stub for wind driven siren on the undercarriage leg (2). Not provided in the Airfix kit, these are simple sprue additions.

Stage 8

I changed my mind as regards markings halfway through the model which accounts for the 'late' modification shown here. For a B1 aircraft (see Les Whitehouse's drawings) the kit exhaust assembly must be removed and replaced by short stubs — I used a biplane strut and sliced it up. (1) Also add a small scoop in front of the leading stack and note that most B-1 machines did not carry gills on the radiator and these are best filled in. This view also affords a look at the siren housing (2) and (modellers should note that the actual 'airscrew' was fairly uncommon) and that wing machine guns have been replaced by thin sprue versions.

Painting

Before anyone shoots me down in flames I have to confess that I'm not 100% happy with the chosen scheme for the Ju87B1 model and would welcome comment from any of the many Luftwaffe experts

out there. References were confusing to say the least but no-one can say the scheme is unattractive! It's 6G+HR of 4/StG1, *Luftflotte 2,* Pas-de-Calais and a photograph of it appears on page 12 of **Aircam's** *Special No. S11* (Volume 2). The star of the comet's tail (if that's what it is), does not appear but I have added it for effect and modellers will find these markings on **Microscale's** 72-16 sheet. Kit decals are good and can be used although I chose replacements such as Microscale for Luftwaffe codes and **Letraset** sheets M3, M4 and M6 for fin, fuselage and wing respectively.

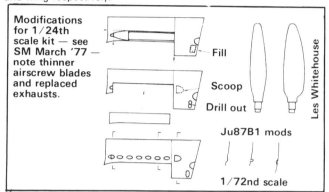

Modifications for 1/24th scale kit — see SM March '77 — note thinner airscrew blades and replaced exhausts.

Fill
Scoop
Drill out

Ju87B1 mods

1/72nd scale

Les Whitehouse

Stage 9

Flatten the tyres slightly to create the impression of load (1) and attach the centre line bomb remembering to replace the gross fins with plastic card substitutes (2). Later braces from sprue are added at each fin tip. For a B1 machine a new thinner profile airscrew should be sought (3) and either you can file down the kit part or find a replacement from another kit. Mine was a cut down Ju 88 item — the **Airfix** kit I believe . . .

Stage 10

I decided to saw up the kit canopy slightly and carefully thinned down the exposed edges prior to painting (1). A spare bin for spent cartridges was made from plastic sheet (2) and installed in the rear cockpit; the rearward firing gun had ammunition drums added from scrap before installing inside the rear canopy and thence to the model.

Stage 11

In order to fit into the slots the kit bomb cradle was reduced in width by cutting a small middle section out and then rejoining (1) — usually the cradles were painted semi-gloss black. Note here the modified exhaust stubs (2), and the reader should also be aware that most B.1s featured a curved intake on the starboard side and not the angular B.2 version of the Airfix kit. I removed this and replaced it with a cut down

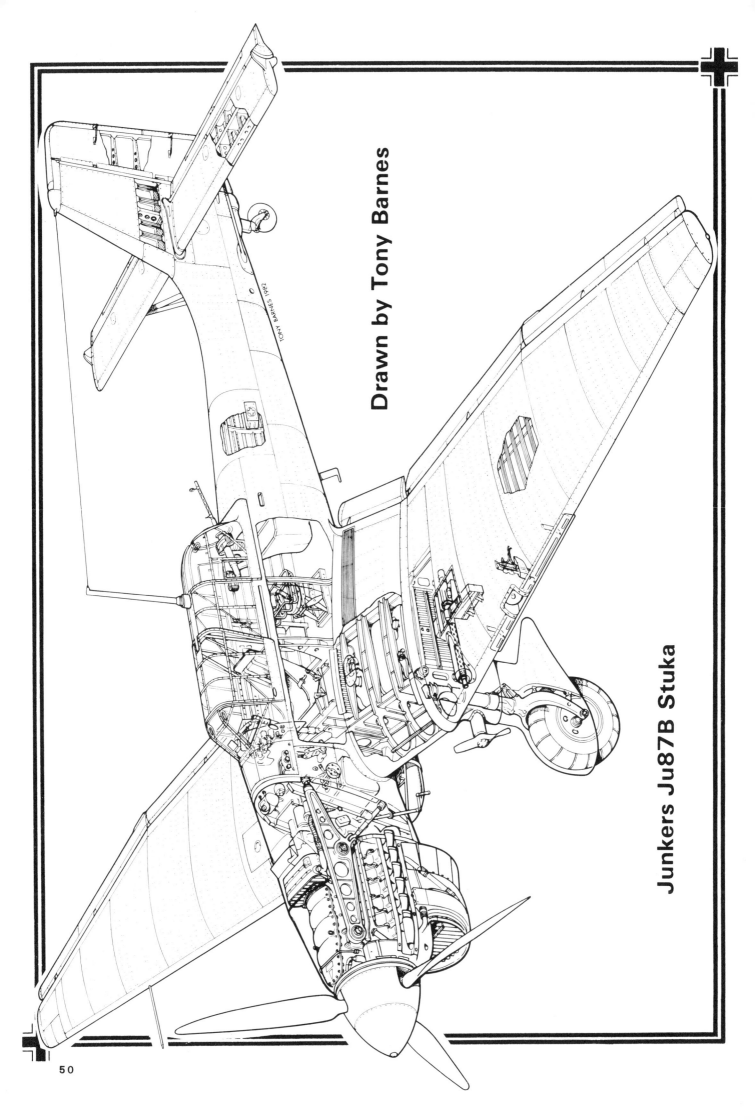

Drawn by Tony Barnes

Junkers Ju87B Stuka

section of an old bomb casing with a grille from scored plastic card installed inside it. Flaps and ailerons require mass balances and 'push rods' and all of these (3) can quite easily be fabricated from stretched sprue and don't forget the horns (4) which will need cutting out and perhaps plastic card replacements are to be preferred.

REFERENCES WE CONSULTED
Cockpit data
The Airfix 1/24th scale kit provided a great reference for cockpit detail as does its instruction sheet but otherwise it's down to *PSL*'s fine book *JU87 Stuka* by *Bruce Robertson* and *Gerald Scarborough*. Fifth of the Classic Aircraft series it will be of enormous value to builders of Airfix Stukas in any scale!

GENERAL DRAWINGS AND MODELLING NOTES
Accurate drawings of the Ju 87B1/2 have yet to materialise but perhaps one day this WW2 classic will get full blown attention by a premier draughtsman — no, we're not making any promises! SCALE MODELS has featured the type in the recent past, noticeably Les Whitehouse who reviewed the 1/24th scale kit in *March* and *April 1977* issues — now out of print. Then of course Neil Robinson reviewed the Airfix 1/72nd version in the *March 1979* issue and discovered, as I did, what a sound model it basically is.

COLOURS
Karl Ries series (for photos) and *Luftwaffe Camouflage and Markings (Vol 2)* by *J. R. Smith* and *J. D. Gallaspy* and reviewed in *SM December 1967*. Also very useful is 'Junkers Ju 87' by *Aero Publishers Inc* of California, and an Italian monograph on the type an Italian monograph on the type 'Ju 87' Stuka by G. Borelli, A. Borgiotti, R. Carina, G. Pini and C. Gori — which may be still available through specialist aviation bookshops. It seems strange that so little reliable reference is available on the Ju 87B but it is hoped that we have been able to assist the modeller in producing a fairly accurate replica of this distinctive dive bomber.   **RLR**

COLOURS AND MARKINGS
ENJOYING considerable success, and terrifying reputation for pin-point accuracy during the *Blitzkreig* campaigns, the Ju 87Bs and Rs of the *StukaGeschwaders* suffered such unacceptable losses during the opening stages of the Battle of Britain at the hands of Fighter Command, that they were effectively withdrawn from operations in mid-August, to return, albeit only briefly, over the British Isles on anti-shipping raids in November 1940.

The Ju 87B/R was finished in a standard uppersurface pattern, two tone green splinter scheme of *Schwarzgrun 70* (**Humbrol** HG15 RFC Green plus a dash of HB1 Dark Green and HU2 Olive Drab 41) and *Dunkelgrun 71* (Humbrol HG2 Dunkelgrun 71 plus a dash of HB8 Dark Slate Grey). Undersurfaces were painted in Hellblau 65 (5 parts Humbrol HG3 Hellgrau 76 plus 2 parts MC12 Prussian Dragoon Blue), the demarcation line between the upper and under surfaces showing some variation around the engine cowling/radiator intake area. Reports of Ju 87B/Rs featuring single shades of green uppersurfaces were probably the result of either the low tonal contrast between *Schwarzgrun 70/Dunkelgrun 71*, giving the impression of a single colour, or, "in the field" repainting in which only one colour was used. Some Ju 87s were also recorded with temporary black undersurfaces, presumably for night operations.

Balkenkreuze were placed in the usual six positions, those on the underside of the wing also being applied across the dive brakes which covered the forward arms of the crosses when folded back in their retracted positions. The *hakenkreuze* (swastikas) were generally located fully on the fin, although many machines still carried them in the earlier, 1939, position, overlapping onto the rudder.

The four digit identification code on the fuselage followed standard practice — the first two digits in black identifying the *Geschwader,* the third digit the individual aircraft letter, normally painted in the staffel colour although there are photographs of Ju87s during this period with the individual aircraft letter merely outlined in the staffel colour, and the fourth digit in black denoting the staffel within the Geschwader. Usually the individual aircraft letter was repeated in black under the wings just outboard of the crosses, but cases of the full code, the original factory radio call sign code, or very occasionally the individual aircraft letter in the staffel colour were not unknown. *Geschwader, Gruppe* or *Staffel* badges were invariably located on the fuselage under the windscreen, with the whole or more usually a part of the spinner, painted in the *Staffel* and/or *Gruppe* colours.

Note in this picture the curved scoop on the engine cowling which replaces the angular item provided with the kit. Other additions include the stub exhausts, scoops grilles to the inside of intakes, and aerial cable from sprue.

Luftwaffe Structure and Markings

DURING the preparation of the colour scheme texts for the Battle of Britain series, we became aware that due to the rather complex and sometimes confusing aspects of Luftwaffe structure and markings, that some form of explanation might be helpful to those modellers not fully conversant with wartime Luftwaffe practice.

The basic Luftwaffe tactical unit was the *Geschwader* (Group). The *Fighter Geschwader*, i.e., *Jagdgeschwader*, abbreviated to JG, consisted of three *Gruppen* (Wings), which in turn was made up of three *Staffeln* (Squadrons). Later on, a fourth and on occasions a fifth, *Gruppe* was added to a *Geschwader*. Also a fourth *Staffel* was added to several *Gruppen*, which caused re-adjustments in the *Staffel* number procedure.

Jagdgeschwader sub-unit breakdown:		
ROTTE	(i.e. leader and wingman)	2 aircraft.
KETTE	(e.g. *Stabskette*)	3 aircraft.
SCHWARM	(e.g. *Stabsschwarm*)	4 aircraft.
STAFFEL	(Squadron)	12 to 14 aircraft.
GRUPPE	(i.e. of three *Staffeln*)	36 to 42 aircraft.
GESCHWADER	(i.e. of three *Gruppen*)	108 to 126 aircraft.

Each *Gruppe* had a *Stabskette* or *Stabsschwarm*, (Staff Flight), as did each *Geschwader*, making a total of some 12 to 16 *Stab* aircraft in a three *Gruppen Geschwader*. The total strength of a *Jagdgeschwader* could have been between 120 to 142 aircraft — on paper. Actual operational strength varied considerably, and the average serviceable figure would obviously have been somewhat lower.

The "in-flight" formations were normally based on the *Schwarm*, spaced out in the classic "finger four" positioning, of two *Rotten* (Fig. 1). In this way, three or four *Schwarme* made a *Staffel*, which formated with other *Staffeln*, up to *Gruppe* strength, usually accompanied by the *Gruppe* and/or *Geschwader Stab* Flights. It was comparatively rare for a full *Geschwader* to fly together 'en masse'. Amongst the reasons for this, was not only would assembling so many fighters together be a time, and fuel consuming operation, but often individual *Gruppen* were based miles apart on different airfields, perhaps with different operational orders such as close escort, or acting as top cover, or even on occasions in the "Frei Jagd" (free hunting) role.

Each *Staffel* was numbered independently within its *Gruppe*, as were the *Gruppen* within their *Geschwader*, (Fig. 2). When written down for administrative purposes however the *Gruppe* number, identified by roman numerals, wasn't mentioned normally, because the *Staffel* number, identified by arabic numerals, indicated to which *Gruppe* the *Staffel* belonged. For example: 9/JG 3 = III *Gruppe*; 3/JG 3 *Gruppe*. Different *Geschwader* however, could only be differentiated between each other by unit badges carried on fuselage sides, usually on the nose in most cases, but occasionally on the rear fuselage as in the case of II/JG 51's aircraft.

Individual aircraft within a *Staffel* were marked with a numeral in the *Staffel* colour, often outlined in a contrasting colour, generally immediately in front of the fuselage cross, although some units positioned the numeral on the nose, e.g. III/JG 27, or under the windscreen, e.g. III/JG 54. An anomaly, not only peculiar to the Battle of Britain but apparent on occasions throughout the war, was the frequent use of black numerals, outlined in either white or red, (also sometimes in yellow), for aircraft of the second *Staffel* in each *Gruppe*, i.e. 2, 5, and 8 *Staffeln*, whose usual colour was red with white trim (Fig. 3). It was also not uncommon for the *Staffelkapitän* to pilot the aircraft marked with the numeral '1', although by July/August this practice tended to be the exception rather than the rule, due to losses and serviceability problems. Another point worthy of mention, is that *Staffel* numerals rarely exceeded the number '16'; aircraft bearing higher numerals tending to indicate that they belonged to a Training *Staffel*.

The different *Gruppen* within a *Geschwader* were identified by a symbol aft of the fuselage cross, (Fig. 4), invariably in the same (*Staffel*) colour as the numerals, exceptions to this being where aircraft had been re-marked with black numerals and had the *Gruppe* symbol left in the original red.

Stab, (Staff Flight), aircraft used a slightly different system of identification, with chevron, bar and/or circle markings in front of the fuselage cross instead of numerals, (Fig. 5). Each combination of chevron, bar and/or circle, ostensibly denoted a particular *Stab* rank, but evidence suggests that in practice the symbols and the *Stab* rank were open to some variation. A further complication, was that not all *Stab* personnel were actually pilots! It was presumably in such cases where there was insufficient *Stab* personnel able to fly, the normal *Staffel* pilots were picked to fly with the *Stabsschwarm*, in numeral marked aircraft such as *Oberleutnant* Wilhelm Frönhofer's "Yellow 10" of *Stab* III/JG 26. *Stab* markings were usually painted in black with white trim, or white with black trim, but examples of black outline only markings have also been recorded. Standard *Gruppe* symbols were generally applied to *Gruppenstab* aircraft, also in black or white with contrasting trim. *Geschwaderstab* aircraft were not allocated any markings aft of the fuselage cross, as they were not attached to any particular *Gruppe* and most *Geschwaderstab* aircraft adhered to this rule, but some, such as the JG2 *Geschwader Kommodore*, Major Helmut Wick's Bf 109E-4, *werke nummer* 5433, (in which he lost his life on the 28th November 1940), and the JG 26 *Geschwader Kommodore*, Major Adolf Galland's E-4, w/n 5819, also circa November 1940, were seen with a horizontal bar aft of their fuselage crosses. However, these exceptions were almost certainly part of both commanders' intepretation of their *Geschwader Kommodore's Stab* rank marking, rather than a (II) *Gruppe* symbol, as both aircraft were also marked with a single chevron and horizontal bar in front of the fuselage cross, (instead of the double chevron and bar), which was the original pre-war marking for a *Geschwader Kommodore*.

In September 1940, an order was issued to the *Jagdgeschwader* to the effect that one *Staffel* in every *Geschwader* was to have its aircraft modified to carry a 250 kilo (550lb) bomb. Instigated as a temporary measure pending the results of trials by the test unit *Erprobungsgruppe* (Erpr.Gr.) 210, operating a mixture of Bf 109Es and Bf 110s, these *Jabo Staffeln* (*Jabo* = Jagdbomber or fighter-bomber) retained standard numeral and *Gruppe* markings. Another unit operating Bf 109Es as fighter-bombers was *Lehrgeschwader* (LG)2. Previously equipped with Henschel Hs 123s in the *Schlacht* or ground attack role, II/(S)LG 2's aircraft introduced the black *Schlacht* triangle marking in front of the fuselage cross, with a coloured *letter*, in the normal *Staffel* colouring combinations, aft of the cross. *Stab* machines carried green coloured letters aft of the cross, and example being *Oberleutnant* Krafft's Green "D" of *Stab* II/(S)LG 2.

I/LG 2's BF 109Es however appear to have retained the normal *Staffel* numeral system, an example being *Uffz*. August Klick's E-7/B

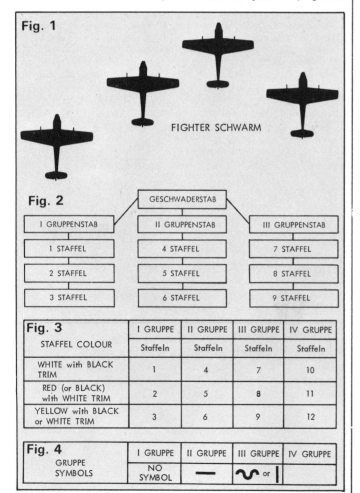

Fig. 1

FIGHTER SCHWARM

Fig. 2

	GESCHWADERSTAB	
I GRUPPENSTAB	II GRUPPENSTAB	III GRUPPENSTAB
1 STAFFEL	4 STAFFEL	7 STAFFEL
2 STAFFEL	5 STAFFEL	8 STAFFEL
3 STAFFEL	6 STAFFEL	9 STAFFEL

Fig. 3 STAFFEL COLOUR	I GRUPPE Staffeln	II GRUPPE Staffeln	III GRUPPE Staffeln	IV GRUPPE Staffeln
WHITE with BLACK TRIM	1	4	7	10
RED (or BLACK) with WHITE TRIM	2	5	8	11
YELLOW with BLACK or WHITE TRIM	3	6	9	12

Fig. 4 GRUPPE SYMBOLS	I GRUPPE	II GRUPPE	III GRUPPE	IV GRUPPE
	NO SYMBOL	—	∿ or |	

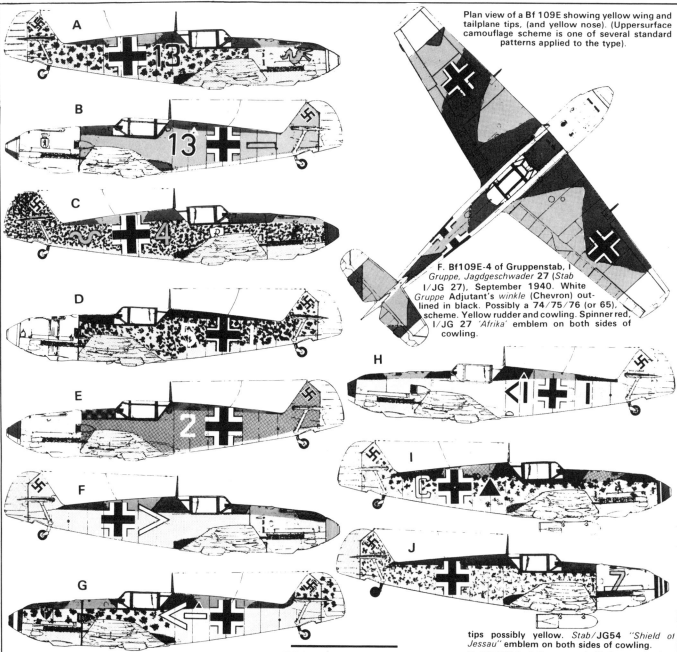

F. Bf109E-4 of Gruppenstab, I *Gruppe, Jagdgeschwader* 27 (*Stab* I/JG 27), September 1940. White *Gruppe* Adjutant's *winkle* (Chevron) outlined in black. Possibly a 74/75/76 (or 65), scheme. Yellow rudder and cowling. Spinner red, I/JG 27 *'Afrika'* emblem on both sides of cowling.

Plan view of a Bf 109E showing yellow wing and tailplane tips, (and yellow nose). (Uppersurface camouflage scheme is one of several standard patterns applied to the type).

ALL DRAWINGS BY NEIL ROBINSON

A. Bf109E- of *Staffel,* I *Gruppe, Jagdgeschwader* 3 (2/JG3), August 1940. Black '13' outlined in white.
71/02/65 scheme with mottled fuselage sides. No mottle on nose area. Yellow top segment on rudder, with yellow wing and tailplane tips. Red *"Tatzelwurm"* (dragon) emblem on both sides of cowling. White spinner with three (or four) yellow concentric rings.

B. Bf 109E-1 of 5 *Staffel,* II *Gruppe, Jagdgeschwader* 27 (5/JG27), September 1940. Black '13' outlined in white, with original red outlined in white, II *Gruppe* horizontal bar.
71/02/65 scheme with very smooth spray of 02 mottle on fuselage sides giving a monotone effect.
Yellow rudder and cowling. Spinner 70 with white segment. *"City of Berlin"* coat of arms, bear emblem, of II *Gruppe* JG27 on port cowling side only.

C. Bf 109E-4 of 8 *Staffel,* III *Gruppe, Jagdgeschwader* 2 (8/JG2). Red '4' and III *Gruppe* wavy bar outlined in white. 71/02/65 scheme with very densely stippled 71 mottle on fuselage sides including fin and rudder.
Spinner either 70 or red. JG2 *"Richthofen"* emblem under cockpit, with 8 *Staffel 'Wolf'* emblem on nose, both sides.

D. Bf 109E-4 of 7 *Staffel,* III *Gruppe, Jagdgeschwader* 53 (7/JG53), September 1940. White '5' and III *Gruppe* vertical bar without any

contrasting outline. 71/02/65 scheme with fairly heavily mottled fuselage sides, (slightly lighter under the cockpit area, on the fin and under the tailplane). Note earlier style, narrow bordered, fuselage cross. White rudder, cowling and spinner. Traces of a red cowling band, peculiar to certain aircraft from all three *Gruppen* of JG 53, faintly visible through white cowling distemper.

E. Bf 109E-4 of 4 *Staffel,* II *Gruppe, Jagdgeschwader* 52 (4/JG52), September 1940. One of the exceptions that proves the rule! White '2' without any contrasting outline and no II *Gruppe* horizontal bar applied, a feature apparently not uncommon amongst II *Gruppe* machines of JG52. 71/02/65 scheme with heavy overspray of 71 on fuselage sides. Yellow rudder and cowling. Spinner 70 with white segment. Red, arched back, *"Cat"* emblem on a white disc on starboard fuselage side immediately in front of windscreen.

G. 109E-4 of *Geschwaderstab, Jagdgeschwader* 54 (*Stab*/JG 54), August 1940. White *Geschwader* 1A Operations Officer's *winkel* and bar marking outlined in black. 71/02/65 scheme with fairly sparse mottling over forward fuselage and tail areas. Spinner 70 with white ring. Wing

tips possibly yellow. *Stab*/JG54 *"Shield of Jessau"* emblem on both sides of cowling.

H. Bf109E-1 of *Gruppenstab,* III *Gruppe, Jagdgeschwader* 26, (*Stab* III/JG26), July 1940. Despite the application of the black *Geschwader* Adjutant's *Winkel* and bar marking, outlined white, it is thought that this machine (*Oberleutnant* Werner Bartlet), was in fact from the *Stab* of III *Gruppe* which would seem to lend weight to the theory that demarcation between *Gruppen* and *Geschwader Stabe* was perhaps not quite as rigid as previously thought.
The black III *Gruppe* bar outlined in white, 71/02/65 scheme. Yellow rudder. Spinner 70, or *Stab* green with white quarter segment. Note smaller than usual fuselage cross, based on a 650mm square rather than the standard size 900mm square.

I. Bf109E-7/B of 6 *Staffel,* II (*Schlacht*) *Gruppe, Lehrgeschwader* 2 (6/II (S) LG2), September 1940. Black *schlacht* triangle with white outline and yellow 'C' outlined in black. 74/75/76 (or 65) scheme with mottling over fuselage sides and fin. Yellow rudder. Spinner 70, with yellow tip and thin white ring. 6 *staffel* emblem on both sides of cowling.

J. Bf109E — 1/B of 9 *Staffel,* III *Gruppe, Jagdgeschwader* 27 (9/JG27), September 1940. Brown, (a colour occasionally used as an alternative to yellow), numeral '7' without a contrasting outline, positioned on the cowling — a practice common to many III/JG27 aircraft. Wings 74/75, solid 75 spine, 76 fuselage sides with 75 mottle, and 65 undersurfaces. Yellow cowling. Brown spinner with three yellow concentric rings.

werke nummer 2058, red '2' of 3/LG 2, shot down on the 15th September 1940. The unit's emblem, a mouse holding an umbrella, was positioned on the rear fuselage of this particular machine, immediately aft of the cross. It will be noted that 2 *Staffel* aircraft should have yellow not red numerals, so it is possible that Klick's Bf 109 was painted with a brown numeral 2 (a colour occasionally used instead of yellow), and not red.

As with the *Jagdgeschwader*, bomber and multi-engined units in the *Luftwaffe* were formed on the *Geschwader*. Several different types of *Geschwader* existed, for which a prefix indicated the unit's role:

KAMPFGESCHWADER (KG) or Bomber Group, (literally, a Battle Group).

ZERSTÖRERGESCHWADER (ZG) or Heavy/Twin engined Fighter Group, (literally a Destroyer Group).

STUKAGESCHWADER (St.G) or Dive Bomber Group.

LEHRGESCHWADER (LG) literally, Operational Training Group, but as has been mentioned previously, LGs were in fact extremely efficient specialist units operating a multitude of aircraft types such as Bf 109Es, Bf 110s, Ju 87s and Ju 88s.

Additional units were formed on the *Gruppe*, being only three to six *Staffeln* in strength, (only one or two *Gruppen* strong):

KAMPFGRUPPE (K.Gr.) or Bomber Wing. *Kampfgruppen* were usually semi-autonomous specialised units, such as K.Gr. 100's pathfinders or K.Gr. 126's minelayers.

AUFKLÄRUNGSGRUPPE (Aufkl.Gr.) or Reconnaissance Wing. Although generally abbreviated to *Aufkl. Gr.*, the type and/or range of reconnaissance the unit was undertaking was indicated by a prefix:

FAGr. *FERNaufklärungsgruppe* or long range/strategic reconnaissance wing.

NAGr. *NAHaulfklärungsgruppe* or short range tactical reconnaissance wing.

HAGr. *HEERESaufklärungsgruppe* or Army Co-operation reconnaissance wing.

When written down, the type and/or range of the unit was indicated as (F), (N), or (H) respectively. For example, 3(F)/22 was the designation for the 3rd *Staffel*, I *Gruppe* of *Fernaufklärungsgruppe* 22.

Aufkl.Gr.Ob.d.L. — Aufklärungsgruppe Oberbefehlshaber der Luftwaffe.

ERPROBUNGSGRUPPE (Erpr.Gr.) or Operational Experimental Wing.

KUSTENFLIEGERGRUPPE (K.Fl.Gr.) or Coastal Reconnaissance Wing.

One additional very important unit which was frequently operational over the British Isles during the 'summer' of 1940, was the *WETTERERKUNDUNGSTAFFEL* (Wekusta) or Meteorological Reconnaissance Squadron!

The sub-unit breakdown for these units was as follows:

KETTE	(e.g. Stabskette)	3 aircraft.
STAFFEL		9 to 12 aircraft.
GRUPPE	(of three Staffeln)	27 to 36 aircraft.
GESCHWADER	(of three Gruppen)	81 to 108 aircraft.

During this particular period, it was normal for *Geschwader* to be only three *Gruppen* strong. However one unit, *Lehrgeschwader* 1, (LG 1), being very much an operational tactics development unit, had two extra *Gruppen*, IV(St.)/LG 1 equipped with Ju 87s and V(Z)/LG 1 with Bf 110s.

Each *Gruppe* had a *Stab* Flight (*Gruppenstabskette*) of three to six aircraft, and each *Geschwader* had a HQ *Stab* Flight (*Geschwaderstabskette*) also of three to six aircraft, making a total of between 12

and 24 *Stab* aircraft in a three *Gruppen Geschwader*. Therefore, the combined total strength of a three *Gruppen Geschwader* could have been anything from 93 to 132 aircraft — once again on paper. Serviceability and combat attrition would have reduced this figure accordingly.

The "in-flight" formations were based on the *KETTE* (Fig. 6), in a 'vic' of 3 aircraft, with three or four *KETTEN* making a *Staffel*, three *Staffeln* making a *Gruppe*, and so on up to *Geschwader* strength.

Bomber and multi-engined units used a four digit number/letter code system on the fuselage sides for identification purposes. To the left of the fuselage cross appeared a number/letter, or letter/number code of two characters, painted in black, which identified the *Geschwader*, eg V4 = KG1, 5K = KG 3, A1 = KG 53, 3Z = KG 77. To the right of the fuselage cross appeared two letters; the first letter, either completely painted in or sometimes just outlined in, the *Staffel* colour (Fig. 7), identified the individual aircraft within its *Staffel*. The second letter, painted black, identified the *Staffel* within its *Gruppe*. For example, V4 + HL (yellow H), would be aircraft 'H' of 3 *Staffel*, I *Gruppe*, KG 1. Staff Flights (*Stabsketten*) followed exactly the same principle, with either medium blue (for *Geschwaderstab*) or bright green (for *Gruppenstab*) individual aircraft letters. The last letter on *Stab* aircraft identified whether the machine was from the *Geschwaderstab* (letter 'A'), or from one of the *Gruppenstabe* (letters B to F — see table). For example V4 + AA (medium blue first) would be aircraft 'A' (the individual aircraft letter 'A' usually indicated the aircraft of the *Geschwader Kommodore*), of the *Geschwaderstabskette* of KG 1 see (Fig. 8).

An occasional exception to the *Staffel/Stab* coloured identification letter rule, which may have been peculiar only to certain units, was the code for *Aufklärungsgruppen*, which, whilst following all other standard Luftwaffe coding practices, did not always paint the individual aircraft letter in the appropriate *Staffel* colour, but painted it black. An example of this was Bf 110 C-5, 5F+ CM, (all characters in black), of 4th *Staffel*, II *Gruppe* /FAGr. 14, forced down almost intact in Sussex on 26th September 1940.

Various combinations of the four digit code system were applied to the undersurfaces of the wings, generally in black, but there were cases where the individual aircraft letter was painted in the *Staffel* colour. Sometimes the whole code was used, with one digit placed on either side of the two wing undersurface crosses, (Fig. 9). However the most common practice was to either paint the individual aircraft letter outboard of both wing under surface crosses, (Fig. 10), or, somewhat rarer, to paint the individual and *Staffel* letters outboard of both wing under surface crosses (Fig. 11); invariably both these two types of presentation were painted in black.

Several types of aircraft, notably Ju87s, Bf 110s, Do 17s and He 111s, were occasionally recorded sporting their individual aircraft letters, in the *Staffel* colours, on the upper surfaces of their wings, generally outboard of the crosses, (Fig. 12). As a further aid to rapid identification during formation flying, some Do 17s, He 111s and Ju 88s were seen with bar symbols, (Fig. 13), painted on the upper surfaces of one, or both, wing tips, and/or on either side of the fin or rudder. It is not thought that these bar symbols referred to the *Gruppe* number, e.g. I *Gruppe*, III *Gruppe*, but were in fact simply formation aids.

Yet another aid to rapid identification of friend from foe, was the liberal use of yellow, and to a somewhat lesser degree white, washable distemper, (easily removable by washing off with aviation fuel). Fighters made the most use of these colours, mainly on the nose area and rudder, but wing and tailplane tips were also sometimes painted. Bombers appear to have been less frequently painted in the distemper, but rudders, and cowling rings especially on Ju 88s, were the most common areas. Propeller spinners, invariably in the factory finish *Schwarzgrun 70*, were prime targets for being overpainted in this distemper, and *Staffel* and/or *Gruppe* colours, for both fighters and bombers as the accompanying illustrations show. □

REFERENCES

KOOKABURRA's "Luftwaffe Camouflage and Markings 1935-45" Vol. 2, by J. R. Smith and J. D. Gallaspy.

Geschwader Kommodore		Gruppe Kommanduer
Geschwader Adjutant		Gruppen Adjutant
Geschwader 1A (Operations Officer)		Gruppen T. O. (Technical Officer)
Geschwader T. O. (Technical Officer)		
Major Beim Stab		**Fig. 5**

Fig. 6

BOMBER/MULTI ENGINED   KETTE

Fig. 7 STAFFEL COLOUR AND IDENTIFICATION LETTERS

STAFFEL	GRUPPEN				
	I	II	III	IV	V
WHITE	1 Staffel = H	4 = M	7 = R	10 = U	13 = X
RED	2 Staffel = K	5 = N	8 = S	11 = V	14 = Y
YELLOW	3 Staffel = L	6 = P	9 = T	12 = W	15 = Z

Fig. 8 STAB COLOUR AND IDENTIFICATION LETTERS

(Medium Blue) A = GESCHWADERSTAB
(Bright Green) B = I GRUPPENSTAB
(Bright Green) C = II GRUPPENSTAB
(Bright Green) D = III GRUPPENSTAB
(Bright Green) E = IV GRUPPENSTAB
(Bright Green) F = V GRUPPENSTAB

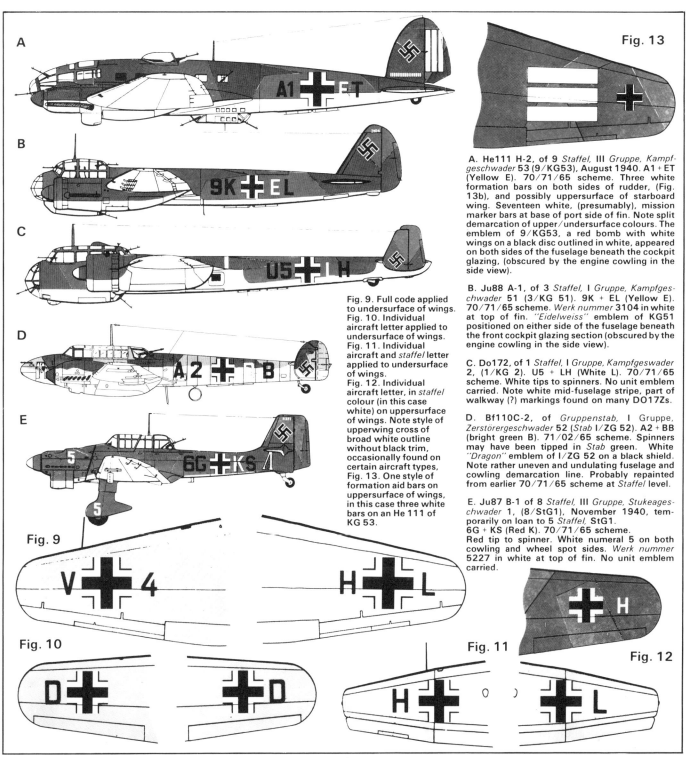

Fig. 13

A. He111 H-2, of 9 *Staffel,* III *Gruppe, Kampfgeschwader* 53 (9/KG53), August 1940. A1 + ET (Yellow E). 70/71/65 scheme. Three white formation bars on both sides of rudder, (Fig. 13b), and possibly uppersurface of starboard wing. Seventeen white, (presumably), mission marker bars at base of port side of fin. Note split demarcation of upper/undersurface colours. The emblem of 9/KG53, a red bomb with white wings on a black disc outlined in white, appeared on both sides of the fuselage beneath the cockpit glazing, (obscured by the engine cowling in the side view).

B. Ju88 A-1, of 3 *Staffel,* I *Gruppe, Kampfgeschwader* 51 (3/KG 51). 9K + EL (Yellow E). 70/71/65 scheme. *Werk nummer* 3104 in white at top of fin. *"Eidelweiss"* emblem of KG51 positioned on either side of the fuselage beneath the front cockpit glazing section (obscured by the engine cowling in the side view).

C. Do172, of 1 *Staffel,* I *Gruppe, Kampfgeswader* 2, (1/KG 2). U5 + LH (White L). 70/71/65 scheme. White tips to spinners. No unit emblem carried. Note white mid-fuselage stripe, part of walkway (?) markings found on many DO17Zs.

D. Bf110C-2, of *Gruppenstab,* I *Gruppe, Zerstörergeschwader* 52 (*Stab* I/ZG 52). A2 + BB (bright green B). 71/02/65 scheme. Spinners may have been tipped in *Stab* green. White *"Dragon"* emblem of I/ZG 52 on a black shield. Note rather uneven and undulating fuselage and cowling demarcation line. Probably repainted from earlier 70/71/65 scheme at *Staffel* level.

E. Ju87 B-1 of 8 *Staffel,* III *Gruppe, Stukeageschwader* 1, (8/StG1), November 1940, temporarily on loan to 5 *Staffel,* StG1. 6G + KS (Red K). 70/71/65 scheme. Red tip to spinner. White numeral 5 on both cowling and wheel spot sides. *Werk nummer* 5227 in white at top of fin. No unit emblem carried.

Fig. 9. Full code applied to undersurface of wings.
Fig. 10. Individual aircraft letter applied to undersurface of wings.
Fig. 11. Individual aircraft and *staffel* letter applied to undersurface of wings.
Fig. 12. Individual aircraft letter, in *staffel* colour (in this case white) on uppersurface of wings. Note style of upperwing cross of broad white outline without black trim, occasionally found on certain aircraft types,
Fig. 13. One style of formation aid bars on uppersurface of wings, in this case three white bars on an He 111 of KG 53.

Fig. 9
Fig. 10
Fig. 11
Fig. 12

''Bf 109 Fuselage Markings 1940'' Books 1, 2 and 3, by Michael Payne.
''Aircraft of the Battle of Britain,'' by William Green.
AIRCAM AVIATION Series:
    S1   Battle of Britain.
    S10 Luftwaffe Bomber Camouflage and Markings 1940.
    S11 Luftwaffe Bomber and Multi-engined Fighter Camouflage and Markings 1940.
    39   Vol. 1 Bf 109.
    42   Vol. 3 Luftwaffe Experten.
    43   Vol. 4 Bf 109.
SQUADRON/SIGNAL PUBLICATIONS:
    No. 4   Luftwaffe in Action.
    No. 6.   He 111 in Action.
    No. 16 Ju 88 in Action.
    No. 30 Bf 110 in Action.
''STUKA'' by Richard P. Bateson.
AIR PICTORIAL, September 1965, Battle of Britain article by J. D. R. Rawlings and Peter M. Corbell.

PSL CLASSIC AIRCRAFT:
    No. 2 Bf 109 by Roy Cross, Gerald Scarborough and Hans Ebert.
    No. 5. Ju 87 by Bruce Robertson and Gerald Scarborough.
AERODATA INTERNATIONAL No. 4 Bf 109E, by Peter G. Cooksley.
ARCHIVE Bf 109E, by Francis K. Mason.
''Berühmte Jagdfliefer und ihre Jagdgeschwader,'' by Holger Nauroth.
''Bf 109 at War,'' by Armand van Oshoven.
''Augsburg Eagle,'' by William Green.
''Warplanes of the Third Reich,'' by William Green.
''The Narrow Margin,'' by Derek Wood and Derek Dempster.
HYLTON LACY
    ''German Fighters of World War II,'' by Martin Windrow.
    ''German Bombers of World War II,'' by Alfred Price.
    ''Kampfgeschwader Edelweiss,'' by Wolfgang Dierich;
and with special thanks to Laurie Glover and Michael Payne for all their help.   □

Ju 88A-1

Cannibalising the Airfix and Italeri 1/72nd scale kits

Stage 1

Assemble together both halves of the Airfix kit fuselage (**1**), removing all internal lugs from the cockpit area. Assemble the wings and main nacelle parts of the Italaeri model and when dry remove the tips as shown (**2**). The wheel well apertures will stand correction (**3**), the corners should be squared off and note the rear doors are closed when the undercarriage is extended.

Stage 2

Clean up the wing roots of both fuselage and wings, cutting the tabs from the latter and cementing these major components together; check that dihedral angle before the glue sets. The best available Ju88 plans are to be found in *Aerodata International No. 9, Junkers Ju88A* which is a vital reference for anyone building this model: to 1/72nd scale, both A1 and A-4 versions are shown with all the relevant differences clearly annotated. Check against these when altering the nacelles.

First cut off $\frac{1}{16}$in. from the rear of each assembled 188 nacelle (**1**)

and also the forward portion of the cowling immediately fronting the cooling gills, then saw the latter from the Airfix cowling fronts (**2**). Glue the assemblies together (**3**) and leave to set. Fill in the slots for the tailplane (**4**).

Stage 3

Further modifications involve the fitting out of the cockpit sides (**1**) and floor (**2**) with 10-thou plastic sheet before applying sprue detail. Note that the nacelles have been packed round with **Milliput**, later to be sanded to the correct shape (**3**) — alternatively these areas could be skinned with 5-thou plastic card. Tape (**4**) is vital when cementing the nose together at this point.

Stage 4

The revised tail assembly. The tailplane and elevators from the 188 kit (**1**) are firmly glued in position. The tips need shortening and the balances sorted out by re-cutting and cementing (**2**) — check with the Aerodata drawings first. Fill the fin balance area with plastic sheet (**3**) and make a new rudder (**4**) from plastic card suitably scored to represent fabric tapes — the trim tab is separate. New wing tips are also added using thick plastic card and referring to Aerodata's scale drawings for shape.

Stage 5

Fitting out the cockpit. Seats were modified items from the scrapbox (**1**) and a suitably cut floor added from 10-thou card (**2**) — note the cutouts to view through the lower windows. There is also a cutout above the ventral gondola (**3**) and the kit parts may have to be modified.

Stage 6

Note the undercarriage doors in closed position (**1**) and that the ventral gondola window apertures have been recut (**2**) and opened out (**3**). The stand slot (**4**) is later disguised by a scored 5-thou card section to represent the bomb doors in that area.

Painting

The model is painted to represent 9K+AL of KG51 and is painted in *Dunkelgrun 71/Schwarzgrun 70* splinter pattern on the upper surfaces with *Helblau 65* on the lower — refer to Neil Robinson's colour notes for more data. Insignia is available in both kits but I used items from **Letraset** sheets M3, M4, and M6, the *'Edelweiss'* emblem originating in **Microscale** sheet 72-9. The usual Luftwaffe sheen was portrayed by applying a coat of matt varnish buffed with lead graphic dust.

Stage 7

Cockpit detail is completed by painting and the addition of decals. Note the new floor (**1**) and the folding seat above the ventral gondola (**2**) — this from scrap plastic; seat straps from painted tape.

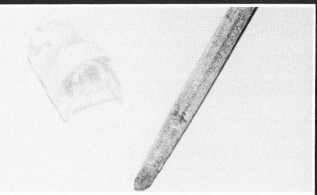

Stage 8

The Airfix Ju88 canopy parts are cemented together and the rear drilled and filed to accept a clear disc for the central MG mounting. Being an A-4 version the kit offers *two* slots but the fitting of the disc hides these most effectively.

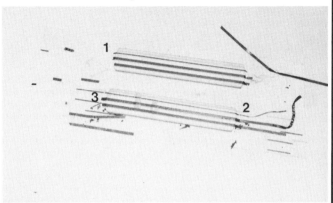

Stage 9

New dive brakes were made from 10-thou clear plastic sheet, (**1**). Letraset lines are applied over the sheet (**2**) in order to act as a mask when the whole unit is painted. Mount the 'brakes' on double sided tape and later carefully remove the masking Letraset to reveal the 'fretted' unit.

Stage 10

The ventral gondola 'canopy' can be trimmed and cemented in the dropped position (**1**) and note the new windows from clear plastic sheet (**2**). Replacement undercarriage doors (**3**) are 10-thou card and incidentally the complete undercarriage units including wheels are pure 188. The painted dive brake is in position, attached by three small plastic sheet brackets (**4**). Ailerons are modified by filling in the trim tabs, and a single one cut from the port aileron — note the plastic card actuating rods for ailerons (**5**) and flaps (**6**). Bombs came from the scrap box (**7**) and will need fin braces from sprue.

REFERENCES WE CONSULTED
Cockpit Data

The aforementioned Aerodata volume is a recommended source for cockpit detail. Also *Junkers Ju88 in Action* published by *Squadron/Signal Publications* and distributed in UK by *Arms and Armour Press Ltd.*

GENERAL DRAWINGS AND COLOUR NOTES

Again the *Aerodata* volume is the source for both 1/72nd scale drawings and colour views. For colour schemes refer to the *Karl Ries* series (photos) and *Luftwaffe Camouflage and Markings (Vol 2)* by JD Gallospy and JR Smith as reviewed in SCALE MODELS December 1977. Colour profiles for the Ju88 will appear in our *September* issue along with the Dornier Do17Z to conclude this series.

COLOURS

THE most modern and fastest of the twin-engined medium bombers used by the *Luftwaffe* in the Battle of Britain, the Ju 88 had literally only just entered operational service a mere few months before the Battle of France. About sixteen bomber *Gruppen* were equipped with the type, mainly in its A-1 form by September 1940, and it was a machine well liked by its crews.

Uppersurfaces were finished in *Schwarzgrun 70/Dunkelgrun 71* in the standard splinter pattern, with *Hellblau 65* undersurfaces (see paint mix guide). Identification letters followed normal *Luftwaffe* practice, with the letter/number, number/letter code to the left of the fuselage cross (in black), denoting the *Geschwader*; the first letter to the right of the cross, either fully painted in, or outlined in, the *Staffel* colour, denoting the individual aircraft within the *Staffel*; and the last letter (in black), identifying the *Staffel* within the *Geschwader*. (See the Luftwaffe Structure and Markings feature in the *April* 1980 issue of SCALE MODELS).

For night operations, a temporary coat of black distemper was applied to many aircrafts' undersurfaces, often extending onto the fuselage sides or in some cases, over all the machine. National insignia and coloured individual aircraft letters were often toned down, also by a thin wash of black.

White formation air bars were to be seen rarely on Ju 88's, but at least one machine, from *KG 77*, has been recorded with one applied to either side of the fin, obliterating part of the swastikas.

The Ju 88's bomb load was usually carried externally, on four streamlined racks inboard of the engine nacelles, although an internal bomb bay was incorporated into the forward fuselage, which was also occasionally used to accommodate an extra fuel tank for long range missions.

The colour of externally carried bombs was generally *Hellblau 65*, but cases of *Dunkelgrun 71* and *Grau 02* bombs were not unknown. The type of bomb was denoted by thin coloured bars between the weapon's fins, or occasionally the whole of the tail cone between the fins was painted in the appropriate colour.

Ju 88's (as well as He 111's and Do 17's), were sometimes to be seen with white-walled tyres, but whether this was carried out by individual crews or a finish applied by certain factories is unknown.

The defensive rear armament of one 7.9mm MG 15 machine gun was sometimes augmented by extra MG's, fitted through the side panel glazing, and a later modification involved a slight re-design of the rear cockpit panels to allow two MG 15's to be accommodated, a feature subsequently incorporated onto the totally re-designed bulged rear canopy of the Ju 88A-4.

Paint mixes:
Schwarzgrun 70: HUMBROL HG 15 RFC Green plus a dash of HB 1 Dark Green and HU 2 Olive Drab, or, *GLOY A340 RLM Schwarzgrun 70*.
Dunkelgrun 71: HUMBROL HG 2 *Dunkelgrun 71* plus a dash of HB 8 Dark Slate Grey, or, *GLOY A341 RLM Dunkelgrun 71*.
Hellblau 65: 5 parts HUMBROL HG 3 *Hellgrau 76* plus 2 parts MC 12 Prussian Dragoon Blue, or, *GLOY A342 RLM Hellblau 65*.
Grau 02: HUMBROL HG6 *Grau 02*, or, *GLOY A343 RLM Grau 02*.

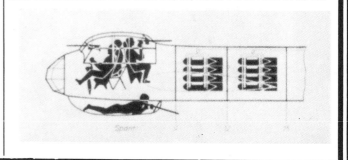

AIRCRAFT ARCHIVE
INDEX TO THE SERIES

Bf 109E

Modifying the 'MATCHBOX' kit

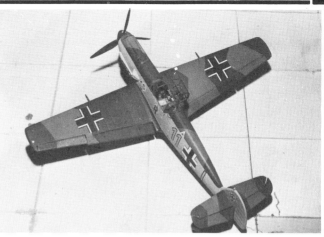

Above: author's completed model suitably modified as described in the text. Right: view of RAF Museum 109E cockpit affords some detail but builders are referred to ASP Plan Pack 2790 where complete cockpit data is provided for the Emil.

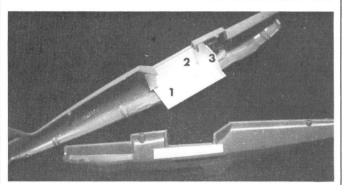

STAGE 1

In an understandable attempt to keep their *Emil* at a reasonable cost "MATCHBOX" have provided the barest of internal details, yet if the canopy is to be modelled open I recommend a serious attempt be made to detail the cockpit. Start by cleaning up the inside of both fuselage halves, thinning cockpit sills particularly. Add a floor (1) and side panels (2) from 10 thou plastic card with a forward 'bulkhead' (3) while you are in the mood. The side panels should follow the natural curve of the fuselage and end flush to the floor.

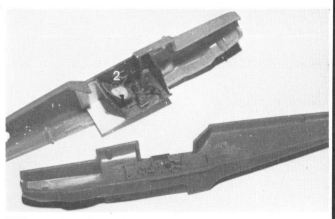

Milliput and suitably sanded, whilst rudder pedals and control column are carefully shaped plastic scraps. Note trim wheels (2). Leave to dry thoroughly before cementing halves together.

STAGE 2

Just how far overboard you go with cockpit detail in this scale depends to some extent on determination and the sources, or lack thereof, at your disposal. In the photograph can be seen the new seat (1) from the scrapbox, mounted on a peg of plastic to raise it above floor level and two trim wheels (sprue) mounted to its port side. The bulkhead behind the seat is 10 thou card (2) and also seen is the oxygen regulator complete with pipe (3). The plastic sheet cockpit sides (4) are further detailed using scraps of sprue and sheet. If you have access to an **Airfix** 1/24th scale Bf 109E kit or a completed model it will offer a useful reference, otherwise a study of reliable publications (quoted elsewhere) is to be recommended.

STAGE 3

Having applied as much detail as possible, note that the instrument panel is applied later, the interior can be given a coat of RLM Grau 02 then 'highlighted' in a lighter shade to bring out all that extra work in relief. Here a parachute pack (1) has been added, shaped from

STAGE 4

The mainplanes can be improved by thinning down all edges and blanking off the wheel wells. And a section of 10 thou card (1) to the inside surface of each upper wing half. Ailerons can be sawn out and

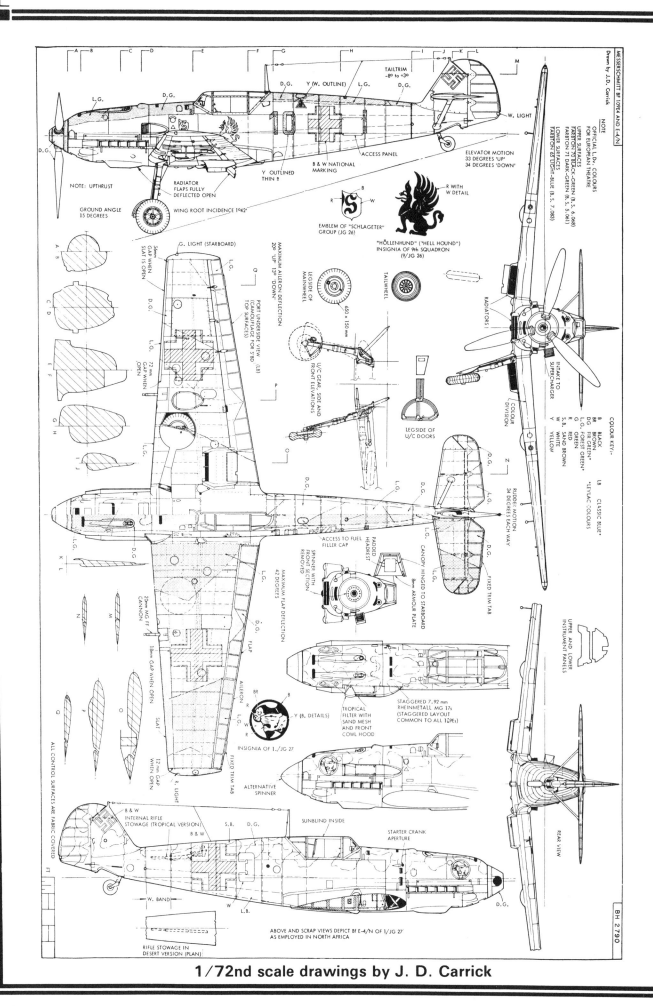

MESSERSCHMITT BF 109E4 AND E-4/N

Drawn by J.D. Carrick

TAILTRIM -8° to +3°

D.G. Y (W. OUTLINE) L.G. D.G.

L.G. D.G.

NOTE
OFFICIAL L.DV. COLOURS
FOR EUROPEAN THEATRE
UPPER SURFACES
FARBTON 70 BLACK-GREEN
FARBTON 71 DARK-GREEN (B.S. 6.068)
FARBTON 71 DARK-GREEN (B.S. 5.061)
LOWER SURFACES
FARBTON 65 LIGHT-BLUE (B.S. 7.083)

W. LIGHT

ELEVATOR MOTION
33 DEGREES 'UP'
34 DEGREES 'DOWN'

ACCESS PANEL

B & W NATIONAL MARKING

Y OUTLINED THIN B

NOTE: UPTHRUST

RADIATOR FLAPS FULLY DEFLECTED OPEN

GROUND ANGLE 15 DEGREES

WING ROOT INCIDENCE 1°42'

EMBLEM OF "SCHLAGETER" GROUP (JG 26)

"HÖLLENHUND" ("HELL HOUND") INSIGNIA OF 9th SQUADRON (9/JG 26)

R WITH W DETAIL

D.G.

RADIATORS

INTAKE TO SUPERCHARGER

COLOUR KEY:-
B   BLACK
BR   BROWN
DG   FIR GREEN*
L.G. "FOREST GREEN"
G   GREEN
R   RED
S.B. SAND BROWN
W   WHITE
Y   YELLOW

LB   CLASSIC BLUE "LEYLAC" COLOURS

COLOUR DIVISION

RUDDER MOTION 34 DEGREES EACH WAY

G. LIGHT (STARBOARD)

56mm GAP WHEN SLAT IS OPEN

MAXIMUM AILERON DEFLECTION 20° 'UP' 13° 'DOWN'

PORT UNDERSIDE VIEW (CAMOUFLAGE FOR S'BD TOP SURFACES) (LB)

LEGSIDE OF MAINWHEEL

TAILWHEEL

650 × 150 mm

U/C GEAR, SIDE AND FRONT ELEVATIONS

LEGSIDE OF U/C DOORS

72mm GAP WHEN OPEN

ACCESS TO FUEL FILLER CAP

PADDED HEADREST

CANOPY HINGED TO STARBOARD

8mm ARMOUR PLATE

FIXED TRIM TAB

SPINNER WITH FRONT SECTION REMOVED

UPPER AND LOWER INSTRUMENT PANELS

MAXIMUM FLAP DEFLECTION 42 DEGREES

20mm MG FF CANNON

18mm GAP WHEN OPEN

FLAP

AILERON

SLAT

TROPICAL FILTER WITH SAND MESH AND FRONT COWL HOOD

INSIGNIA OF 1./JG 27

Y (B. DETAILS)

STAGGERED 7.92 mm RHEINMETALL MG 17s (STAGGERED LAYOUT COMMON TO ALL 109Es)

ALTERNATIVE SPINNER

FIXED TRIM TAB

R. LIGHT

12mm GAP WHEN OPEN

B & W INTERNAL RIFLE STOWAGE (TROPICAL VERSION)

B & W

SUNBLIND INSIDE

STARTER CRANK APERTURE

S.B. D.G.

W. BAND

L.B.

W

REAR VIEW

D.G.

ALL CONTROL SURFACES ARE FABRIC COVERED

ABOVE AND SCRAP VIEWS DEPICT Bf E-4/N OF 1/JG 27 AS EMPLOYED IN NORTH AFRICA

RIFLE STOWAGE IN DESERT VERSION (PLAN)

BH 2 790

1/72nd scale drawings by J. D. Carrick

reattached at a different attitude if desired (2) and so can the flaps if required to be drooped.

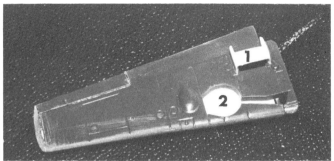

STAGE 5

I was none too happy with the underwing radiator baths as supplied by "MATCHBOX" and accordingly sought alternatives. None were available so plastic card replaced the rather undernourished kit items. I built them up for 20 thou (1) plastic card using available scale drawings for reference. 'grilles' of 10 thou were fitted inside them, covered with a piece of fine silk then painted dark grey *thinly* applied. If carefully drybrushed with dull metallic grey a fine mesh effect can result. Blanked wheel wells can be seen in the picture (2).

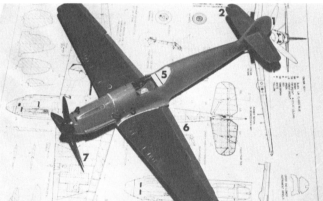

STAGE 6

Assembly now follows kit instructions for a while and if you wish to saw and re-angle the tail control surfaces (1) and (2) now is the time. Improvements at this stage include filler (3) on wing and fuselage joints plus filing out two cowling slots forward of the gun troughts (4). Rear fuselage and 'shelf' (5) have been added from 10 thou card. also note drooped flaps (6).

A replacement airscrew and spinner was called for (7) and as I happened to have a spare from the **Hasegawa** *Emil* available this was used instead.

STAGE 7

Next add an ETC 500 bomb rack (if your chosen subject requires it) and the centre line channel from sprue (1) having smoothed over the wing/fuselage joints. The fuselage radiator bath needs improving by cutting out the slot (2), scoring in the flap and adding a Matrix inside as we did for the wing rads. Do not forget the cooling slot immediately aft of the spinner (3) which can be filed out. Here can be seen the twin wing radiator baths with rear flaps dropped down thus clearing the already drooped wing flaps (4). The rear portion of the "MATCHBOX" baths *(parts 30* and *31)* can be cut off, reshaped and cemented to the flaps at this stage.

Painting

I found a fairly attractive and simple scheme for the model in PSL's Bf 109E book on page 49 — a Bf 109E-4/B (W Nr 3259) of *9 Staffel/JG26* and flown by *Uffz* Braun late in 1940. The colours of *Helblau 76, Dunklegrun 71* and *RLM Grau 02* were mixed in accordance with Neil Robinson's specifications set out below. The camouflage pattern is based on *two* distinct styles seen during the period, that depicted in Steve Archibald's colour plate being the more common of the two.

With the exception of the *red* JG26 *Hollen-hund* insignia which was a **Microscale** sheet No *72-9* item, all markings were taken from the **Letraset** dry pressure range still available from **BMW Models**. Sheets *M4, M6* and *M25* provided national insignia while sheets *M29* and *M38* yielded the number 11 and *Gruppe* symbol, sheet *M8*, the 'S' *'Schlageter'* badge. Stencil detail was both handpainted and taken from items found in the scrap decal box before a coat of semi-matt varnish was applied overall completing the basic paintwork. Detail colouring includes the wheel wells, *RLM Grau* 02, with light brown sides to represent the fabric shields, gloss black wheel hubs and dark grey tyres, the spinner and airscrew in *Schwarzgrun 70,* the blade roots in dull metal.

Wheel well and radiator bath detail. Note museum example lacks the usual zip-up canvas covering for the wheel well walls.

STAGE 8

A new instrument panel was made from 10 thou card painted *66 Schwarzgrau* (Mix Humbrol *67/M22 Tank Grey* plus a dash of *HB6 Sea Grey Medium* or *Gloy M39* (one part) plus a spot of *M40*) with various dials from scrap decal sheets. Seat straps are fabricated from painted tape strips with the armour plate of the canopy fashioned from 5 thou plastic card. The canopy itself was sawn into three, the edges being thinned by careful paring with a *sharp* craft knife before painting. Attach to the model with PVA adhesive.

"MATCHBOX" do not provide any bombs with their kit (though Airfix does) so it is down to another hunt in the scrap box for a scale 250kg bomb. If not readily to hand, a piece of dowel or plastic rod 3/16" in diameter will have to be carved to shape and 10 thou card fins attached. The bomb is painted *Hellblau 76* with a yellow band on the rear casing centrally between each fin. Sprue bomb shackles complete this area.

Final details include aerial wire (sprue) navigation lamps (**Kristal Kleer**) and 5 thou card trim tabs for ailerons, elevators and rudder which should be painted *23 Rot* (Humbrol *60/M12 Scarlet* plus a dash of *34/M10 white* or Gloy *M46* (one part) to a spot of *M40*). This same colour is also used for stencil detail and no-tread lines on upper wing surfaces.

REFERENCES WE CONSULTED

COCKPIT DETAIL

Messerschmitt Bf 109, versions B-E, by *Roy Cross* and *Gerald Scarborough* in collaboration with *Hans J Herbert.* Published by *PSL* in conjunction with Airfix Products Ltd this fine book can be firmly recommended for all modellers of the *Emil.* Scores of photos and diagrams aid modellers in building and detailing the 1/24th scale. Airfix Superkit only, but all Bf109E modellers can benefit from the material included. Reviewed SM *December* 1972.

Aerodata International No. 4

Providing some large area and thus more useful, reference photographs, colour side views and good graphic cockpit sketches as well as 1/72nd scale drawing, this monograph by *Peter Cooksley* is of much value. Reviewed SM *May 1979.*

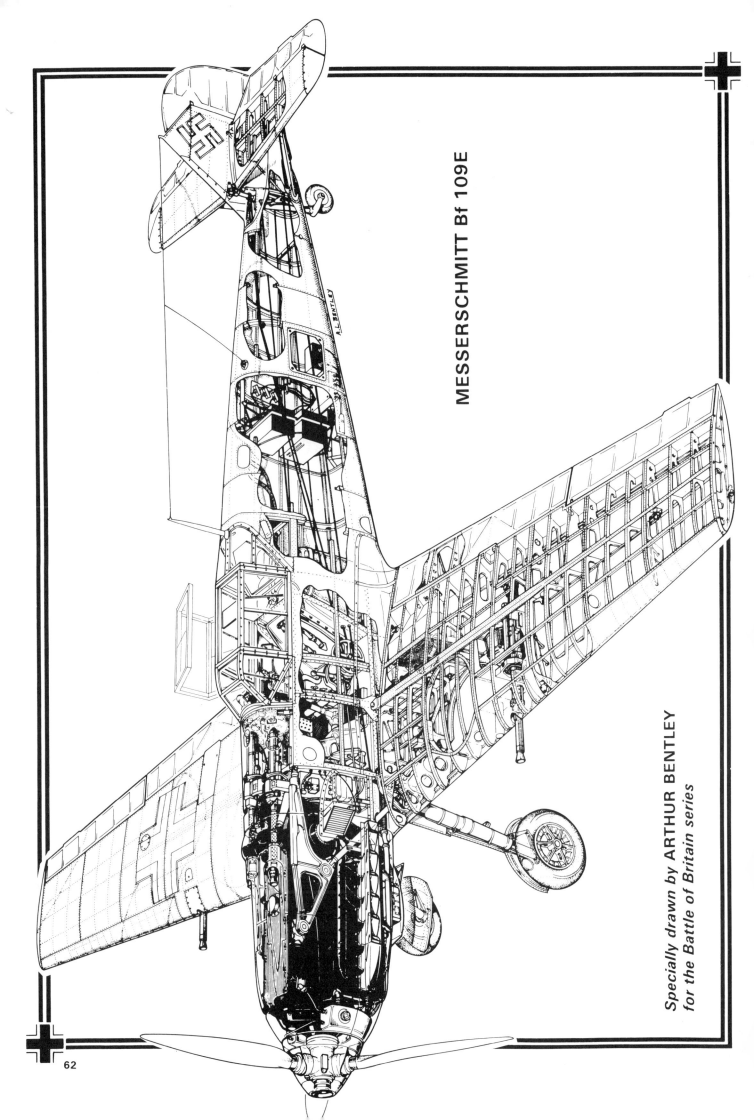

MESSERSCHMITT Bf 109E

A.L. BENTLEY

*Specially drawn by ARTHUR BENTLEY
for the Battle of Britain series*

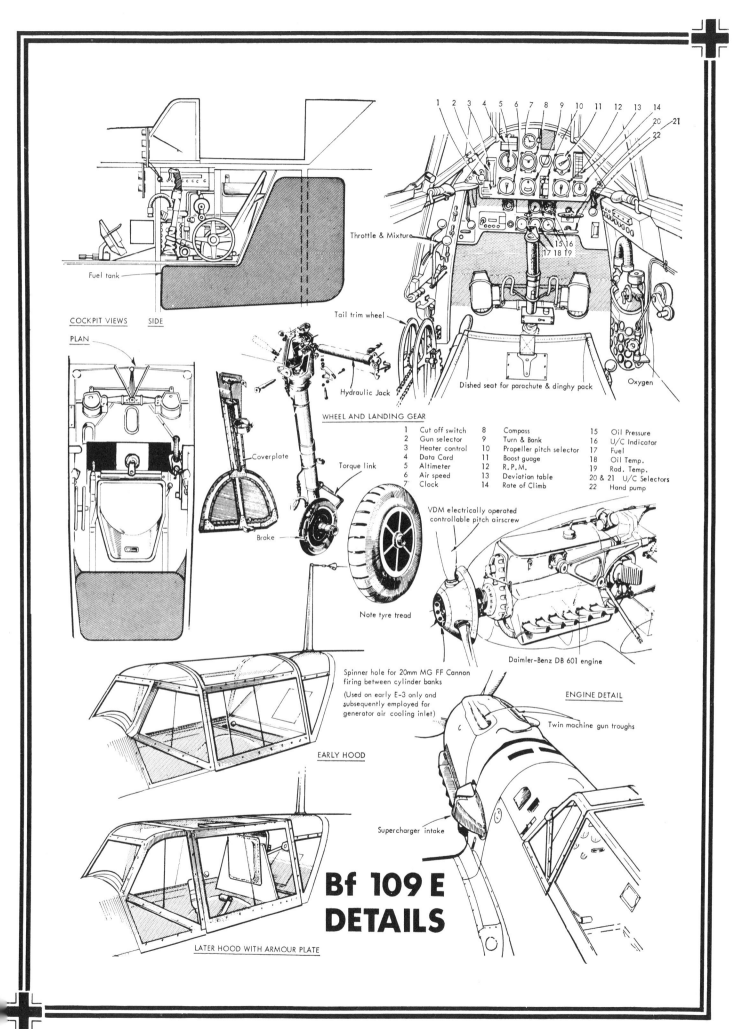

COCKPIT VIEWS SIDE

PLAN

Fuel tank

Throttle & Mixture

Tail trim wheel

Dished seat for parachute & dinghy pack

Oxygen

Hydraulic Jack

WHEEL AND LANDING GEAR

Coverplate

Torque link

Brake

Note tyre tread

1	Cut off switch	8	Compass	15	Oil Pressure
2	Gun selector	9	Turn & Bank	16	U/C Indicator
3	Heater control	10	Propeller pitch selector	17	Fuel
4	Data Card	11	Boost guage	18	Oil Temp.
5	Altimeter	12	R.P.M.	19	Rad. Temp.
6	Air speed	13	Deviation table	20 & 21	U/C Selectors
7	Clock	14	Rate of Climb	22	Hand pump

VDM electrically operated
controllable pitch airscrew

Daimler-Benz DB 601 engine

Spinner hole for 20mm MG FF Cannon
firing between cylinder banks

(Used on early E-3 only and
subsequently employed for
generator air cooling inlet)

ENGINE DETAIL

Twin machine gun troughs

EARLY HOOD

Supercharger intake

Bf 109 E
DETAILS

LATER HOOD WITH ARMOUR PLATE

GENERAL DRAWINGS AND MODELLING NOTES

No 4, there are our own set of scale drawings, drawn and re-searched by J. D. Carrick and R. G. Moulton, including cockpit sketches, available as plan pack 2790 from SCALE MODELS PLANS SERVICE. The pack includes drawings to 1/24th, 1/48th and 1/72nd scale. Also refer to SM *December 1969* issue for 109E references and SM *February 1972* for modelling data and reference notes and sketches by the late *Bob Jones*.

SCALE MODELS May 1976

Harry Woodman provides plenty of useful modelling data by explaining how to create an *accurate* Bf109E to 1/48th scale from the old **Monogram** kit. Many useful tips applicable also to 1/72nd scale versions can be found in this feature.

COLOURS

Karl Ries series (for photos) and **Luftwaffe Camouflage and Markings (Vol 2)** by *JR Smith* and *JD Gallaspy* published by *Kookaburra* and reviewed in SM *December 1976*. Also useful were the various articles on Bf 109E colour schemes and markings circa late 1939 to late 1940 by *Michael Payne* and published in *Ron Firth's* **PAM News Nos 11, 13, 15, 21,** and **23.** Another source is **Luftwaffe Fighter Units, Europe 1939-41** by *Jerry Scutts,* published by *Aircan/Airwar* and reviewed in the SM *November 1977*. It includes many useful photos and colour plates.

COLOURS AND MARKINGS

DURING the invasion of France and the Low Countries in the spring of 1940, it was noticed that many Bf109E's had adopted a revised colour scheme, which included the repainting of the black-green *Schwarzgrun 70* (**Humbrol** *HG15 RFC Green* plus a dash of *HB1 Dark Green* and *HU2 Olive Drab 41)* areas with the lighter grey-green *Grau 02* (Humbrol *HG6 RLM Grau 02).* The pale grey-blue *Hellblau 65* (5 parts Humbrol *HG3 Hellgrau 76* plus two parts *MC12 Prussian Dragoon Blue)* undersurface colour was extended up the fuselage sides onto a line level with the canopy sill, and entirely covered the fin and rudder. Spinners generally remained in *Schwarzgrun 70,* or *Dunkelgrun 71* (Humbrol *HG2 Dunkelgrun 71* plus a dash of *HB8 Dark Slate Grey).*

National insignia had also gone through a change. The fuselage and underwing *Balkenkreuze* received wider white borders, and the *Hakenkreuz* was repositioned onto the fin from its previous location centrally across the fin and rudder hinge line.

None of these changes were effected overnight, there being evidence to suggest that 71/02/65 finished Bf 109E's were operational shortly after the fighting in Poland had ceased, and certainly the scheme was in fairly widespread use before the 1940 "Blitzkrieg" offensive, as contemporary photographs taken in the rather cold early spring show.

By the time of the opening stages of the Battle of Britain, 70/71/65 finished Bf 109E's were the exception, and the 71/02/65 scheme was firmly established, albeit with minor variations and additions. The large areas of the light grey-blue *Hellblau 65* fuselage sides was obviously too conspicuous for some units, who covered these areas with mottles of various depths and colours, usually permutations of 70, 71 and 02.

Presumably because of spending much of its flying time over the

Channel and requiring a suitable 'over water' camouflage, the introduction of the three 'mid-war' fighter greys on Luftwaffe fighters appears to have occured much earlier than had previously been thought. These greys consisted of dark grey *Dunkelgrau 74* (Humbrol *HG4 Dunkelgrau 74)* and medium grey *Mittelgrau 75* (3 parts Humbrol *HG4* plus 1 part *34/M10 White)* uppersurface colours, with light blue-grey *Hellgrau 76* (Humbrol *HB4 Duck Egg Blue* plus a dash of *34/M10 White)* for the undersurfaces.

A mixed assortment of colours from the existing green shades and the new grey shades was not uncommon; wing and tailplane upper-surfaces in 71/02 and the fuselage spine in 74/75, or just one of these colours, being a frequent variation. Even when the upper-surfaces were entirely repainted in 74/75 over the 71/02, the original *Hellblau 65* undersides were often retained.

70/02/65 was still the predominant scheme throughout the Battle of Britain period, but as the summer passed into autumn, and autumn into winter, the percentage of 74/75/76 (or 65) finished *Emils* increased, although it was not until the November 1941 issue of the L Dv 521/1 camouflage manual that the official use of 74/75/76 was promulgated.

Unlike the RAF's system of code letters, Luftwaffe single engined fighters carried coloured numerals and *Gruppe* symbols for identi-fication purposes. As it is not intended to go into the *Jagdgeschwader* structure and markings systems in this particular series of articles, it must suffice to say that the numerals and *Gruppe* symbols followed closely a specific colour code, although the inevitable variations did occur. *Geschwader, Gruppe,* and/or *Staffel* badges were also an integral part of the Bf 109E's markings, but as the Battle continued it was realised that some form of instant recognition of friend from foe was needed.

Yellow, *Gelb 04* (10 parts Humbrol *24/M15 Trainer Yellow* plus 1 part *HM10 Scarlet)* or, white *Weiss 21* cowlings and rudders were the most common instant identification features, but spinners, wingtips and even tailplane tips came under the painter's spray gun.

Bf 110 C-4

Constructing the Monogram 'Zerstörer'

Monogram's Bf110 is an excellent basis for a sound replica and needs relatively little extra detailing. *Photo: R. L. Rimell.*

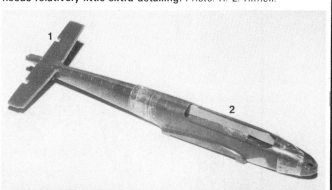

Stage 1

Commence construction by separating ailerons (1) and flaps (2) from all wing components. Score along hinge lines, saw out the gaps and gently bend the parts free, later cleaning up the cut edges. Underwing bomb racks (3) are filed off and the under fuselage belly bomb rack (4) is cut away with a razor saw — this being discarded of course.

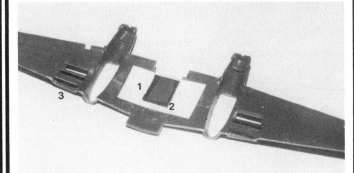

Stage 4

Main assembly is continued with reference to the Monogram instruction sheet and care should be taken to smooth in the 'plug' which has replaced the bomb rack. (1) Re-cement ailerons, elevators and rudders at desired angles; flaps too, but some paring away of the rear nacelle edges may be required first (2). Wheel well walls are from 10 thou plastic card (3) cemented to the sides with liquid cement. Later the excess is removed by knife and cleaned up with wet'n'dry paper.

Stage 2

Fill in the removed bomb rack area by fitting a thick section of plastic card topped by a larger piece to achieve some degree of rigidity to the centre section. (1) Pack out with another smaller piece (2) which will support a new cockpit floor. Radiator grilles (3) have also been added, (from thin plastic card) to provide a 'filled' appearance for the radiator baths.

Stage 3

Fuselage halves securely taped whilst cement dries. The tailplane has been installed but note that the elevators are already removed and balance slots filed out (1). Also just visible, one of the new cockpit sides from 10 thou plastic card (2), all internal pegs having previously been removed from both fuselage halves.

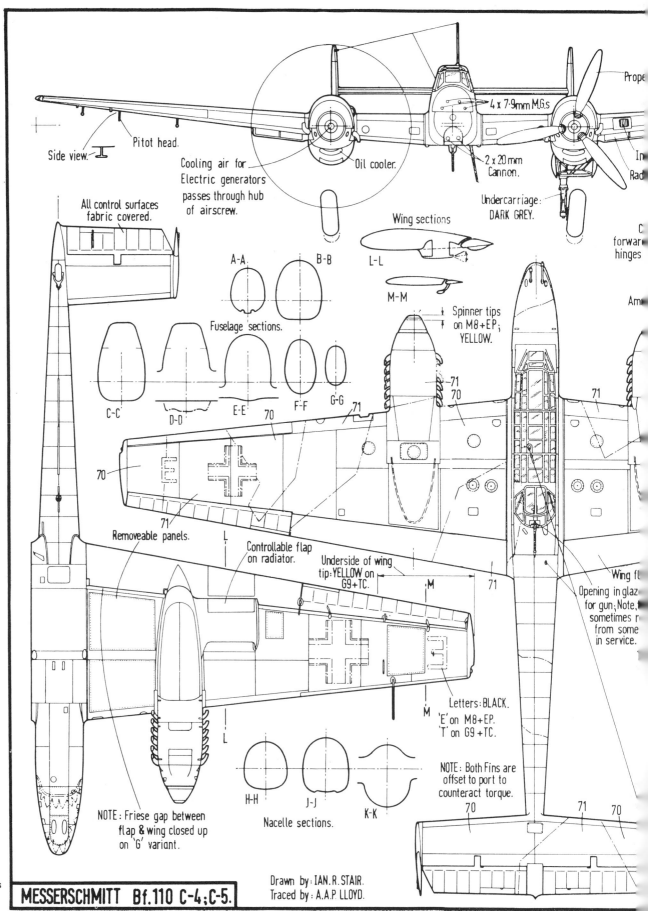

Side view. Pitot head.

Propel

Cooling air for Electric generators passes through hub of airscrew.

Oil cooler.

4 x 7·9mm M.G.s

2 x 20 mm Cannon.

Undercarriage: DARK GREY.

In

Rad

C
forwar
hinges

All control surfaces fabric covered.

Wing sections

L-L

M-M

A-A. B-B

Fuselage sections.

C-C D-D E-E F-F G-G

70 70 71 71

Spinner tips on M8+EP; YELLOW.

-71
70

71

Am

71

Removeable panels.

Controllable flap on radiator.

Underside of wing tip: YELLOW on G9+TC.

M

71

Wing fl

Opening in glaz
for gun; Note,
sometimes r
from some
in service.

L

L

M

Letters: BLACK.
'E' on M8+EP.
'T' on G9+TC.

NOTE: Friese gap between flap & wing closed up on 'G' variant.

H-H J-J K-K

Nacelle sections.

NOTE: Both Fins are offset to port to counteract torque.

70 71 70

MESSERSCHMITT Bf.110 C-4; C-5.

Drawn by: IAN. R. STAIR.
Traced by: A.A.P. LLOYD.

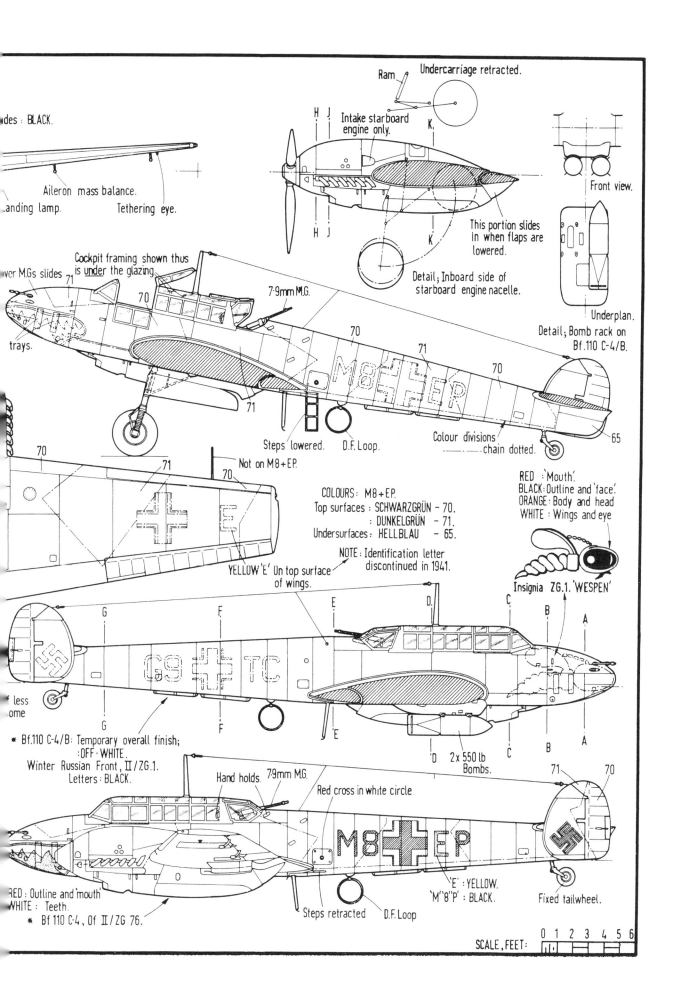

des : BLACK.

Aileron mass balance.
Landing lamp.   Tethering eye.

Undercarriage retracted.
Ram
Intake starboard
engine only.
H J   K
H J   K
This portion slides
in when flaps are
lowered.
Detail; Inboard side of
starboard engine nacelle.

Front view.

Underplan.

Detail; Bomb rack on
Bf.110 C-4/B.

Cockpit framing shown thus
is under the glazing.
over M.Gs slides 71   70   7·9mm M.G.   70   71   70
trays.

M8+EP

Steps lowered.   D.F. Loop.   Colour divisions
chain dotted.   65

70   71   Not on M8+EP.
70

Red cross in white circle.

YELLOW 'E' On top surface
of wings.

COLOURS: M8+EP.
Top surfaces : SCHWARZGRÜN – 70.
: DUNKELGRÜN – 71.
Undersurfaces : HELLBLAU – 65.

NOTE: Identification letter
discontinued in 1941.

RED : 'Mouth'.
BLACK: Outline and 'face'.
ORANGE: Body and head
WHITE : Wings and eye

Insignia ZG.1. 'WESPEN'

G   F   E   D.   C   B   A

G9+TC

less
ome   G   F   E   D   C   B   A

2 x 550 lb
Bombs.

* Bf.110 C-4/B: Temporary overall finish;
: OFF-WHITE.
Winter Russian Front, II/ZG.1.
Letters: BLACK.

Hand holds.   7·9mm M.G.   Red cross in white circle.

M8+EP

RED : Outline and 'mouth'
WHITE : Teeth.
* Bf 110 C-4, Of II/ZG 76.

Steps retracted   D.F. Loop

'E' : YELLOW.
'M''8''P' : BLACK.

Fixed tailwheel.

71   70

SCALE, FEET: 0 1 2 3   4 5 6

Stage 5 *(From previous page)*

Cockpit detail as provided by Monogram is rudimentary and on the subject model new cockpit sides and floor were added using 10 thou plastic sheet (**1**) The kit seat assembly was used (**2**) and extra details are added from plastic sprue and scrap. Note the wing spar (**3**) and observer's seat (**4**) — both from scrap plastic. Note also that the leading edge intake (**5**) has been enlarged, and for absolute realism the cannon slots on the nose underside can be drilled out.

Stage 6

Cockpit detailing is completed by painting *RLM Grau* and then dry-brushing to highlight extra detail. Note decalled instrument panel and side consoles (**1**), a new control column (**2**) from an **Airfix** Stuka, radio (**3**) and seat straps (**4**) the latter out of painted adhesive tape suitably sliced. The model is now ready for the colour scheme.

Painting

The subject model is finished to represent M8+EP of II/ZG 76 and is painted accordingly in *Dunkelgrun 71/Schwarzgrun 70* splinter pattern on the upper surfaces with *Hellblau 65* on the lower. Neil Robinson provides the colour mixes opposite and one is referred to Steve Archibald's colour art at the beginning of this feature for details of the pattern. Kit insignia can be used although I used replacements from **Letraset** sheets M3, M4 and M6 and **Microscale's 72-136** for the sharkmouth which had to be slightly modified by brush after application to the model. It's more than likely that the third staffel colour numeral (E) should also be thinly outlined in white and that the letters under as well as above the wing tips were in the same colour rather than black. The usual Luftwaffe overal sheen was portrayed by rubbing the model with lead graphite dust — also doubling as an effective method of 'weathering' as well.

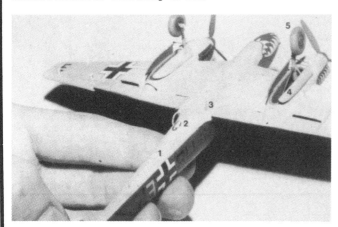

Stage 7

Several extra details can be added on the model's underside including the six short aerial masts (**1**), a DF loop from rolled 5 thou sheet strip (**2**), the trailing aerial fairlead from sprue (**3**) and additional undercarriage leg supports (**4**). Note that both mainwheel 'tyres' have been flattened by gentle heating prior to installation (**5**).

Stage 8

Further modifications involve the cutting apart of the rear canopy in order to re-attach in an open position and thus afford a clearer view

of the interior (**1**). Ammunition racks are scratchbuilt from sprue and a replacement 7.9 MG from an **Italaerei** kit added before the rear canopy is reinstalled together with a new upper 'flap' from clear plastic sheet. Other additions include a scored 10 thou grille to the leading edge intake (**2**) and scrap plastic scissors links to the undercarriage legs. For absolute accuracy the armoured windscreen should be filed away and a flat section of transparent plastic sheet substituted (**3**). Note also 'undercarriage down' indicators from sprue (**4**).

Stage 9

One fairly simple way to pick out the many canopy framelines is by virtue of painted decal strip in this case **Scalemaster** clear film pre-painted in both *70/71* (**1**). The sheet is sliced into thin strips (**2**) and carefully applied to the transparency, exposed edges of the cut rear portion later touched in by brush. Final additions include a rear access ladder and aerial wires — all from finely stretched sprue.

REFERENCES WE CONSULTED

Cockpit data

'*Messerschmitt Bf110*' by *RS Hirsch* and *Uwe Feist* published by *Aero Publishers Inc.* of California and UK distributed by **Argus Books Ltd.**, offers useful cockpit internal while views and details of fitting out a 1/72nd Bf110 interior were published in *Modelworld, December*

Captured Bf110 with all canopy hoods open — careful cutting is needed to reproduce this in 1/72nd. *Photo: Aeroplane.*

1972 by *Les Whitehouse* (see below). Also recommended is 'Messerschmitt Bf110 Zerstorer in Action' by *J. L. Campbell* and *D. Greer* published by *Squadron/Signal USA* and distributed in UK by **Arms and Armour Press.**

GENERAL DRAWINGS AND COLOUR NOTES

SCALE MODELS Plan Pack 2881 offers a set of scale drawings to 1/72nd and 1/48th scales — all major variants are shown and the reprint includes colour notes and reference photos. Also highly recommended are a series of three features by Les Whitehouse which appeared in *Modelworld* magazine in the *October/November 1972* and *December 1973* issues. Full data on additional details and corrections to the then existing Bf110 kits was given plus colour notes and plenty of useful drawings.

COLOURS

The Karl Ries series (for photos) and *Luftwaffe Camouflage and Markings (Vol 2)* by *JR Smith* and *JD Gallaspy* as reviewed in *SM, December 1977,* plus the aforementioned Squadron/Signal Publication.

COLOURS AND MARKINGS

BY the opening stages of the 'Battle', Bf 110's were to be seen in a standard uppersurface splinter pattern of *Schwarzgrun 70 (Humbrol* HG 15 RFC Green + dash of HB1 Dark Green and HU2 Olive Drab 41), and *Dunkelgrun 71 (Humbrol* HG2 *Dunkelgrun 71 +* dash of HB8 Dark Slate Grey), with *Hellblau 65* undersurfaces (5 parts *Humbrol* HG3 *Hellgrau 76* + 2 parts MC12 Prussian Dragoon Blue). However, like the Bf 109E equipped units (see S.M. *December 1979*) a change-over to a lighter scheme, more compatable to the French countryside, had become increasingly more common during the Blitzkreig offensive in the spring of 1940, which replaced the *Schwarzgrun 70* areas with *RLM Grau 02 (Humbrol* HG6 *RLM Grau* 02), and raised the *Hellblau 65* undersurfaces up to the cockpit glazing sill level. Various densities of mottling of *Schwarzgrun 70, Dunkelgrun 71* and *Grau 02* was then applied over the fuselage sides and both sides of the fins, which had also received a base coat of *Hellblau 65.* Once again, like the Bf 109E's, the introduction of the 'greys' *Dunkelgrau 74 (Humbrol* HG4 *Dunkelgrau 74)* and *Mittelgrau 75* (3 parts *Humbrol* HG4 plus 1 part 34/M10 White) uppersurfaces began during the middle stages of the 'Battle'. Undersurfaces/Fuselage/fin sides initially remained in *Hellblau 65,* or, as was later to become standard, repainted in *Hellgrau 76 (Humbrol* HB4 Duck Egg Blue + dash of 34/M10 White). Fuselage/fin side mottling consisted of greys 74 and 75 and 70.

Although technically a fighter type, the Bf 110 adopted bomber style unit markings which consisted of a number/letter, letter/number combination, in black, denoting the *Geschwader,* to the left of the fuselage cross, with two letters to the right of the cross. The first letter to the right of the cross, was either completely painted in, or simply outlined in, *Staffel* colour and identified the individual aircraft within the *staffel.* The last letter, in black, identified the staffel within the Geschwader.

The individual aircraft letter was normally repeated, in black, or the *staffel* colour under the wing tips outboard of the crosses, but cases where the full code was applied were not unknown. Some units applied the individual aircraft letter on the uppersurfaces of the extreme wing tips, outboard of the crosses, in the *staffel* colour, but this was not general practice for the type. The factory finished *Schwarzgrun 70* painted propeller spinners were the main areas for painting in the *Gruppe* and/or *Geschwader* colours, although the nose cone was also recorded as being overpainted in some instances. *Staffel, Gruppe* or *Geschwader* badges were invariably applied to the nose, either directly under, or forward of, the pilot's windscreen.

SELECTED FURTHER READING

This list has been compiled with the kind co-operation of the Royal Air Force Museum, Hendon.

The Battle of Britain Then and Now Mk V, Ramsey. 'After the Battle' Magazine, £39.95.

The Blitz Then & Now, Vol 1, Ramsey, ATB Magazine, £23.50.

The Blitz Then & Now, Vol 2, Ramsey, ATB Magazine, £37.50.

The Blitz Then & Now, Vol 3, Ramsey, ATB Magazine, £37.50.

The Battle of Britain: The Jubilee History, Hough/Richard, Hodder, £16.95.

RAF Squadrons in the Battle of Britain, Robinson, Cassell, £12.95.

Battle of Britain: The Forgotten Months, Foreman, Air Research, £14.95.

Fight for the Sky, Halpenny, Patrick Stephens Ltd, £6.95.

Strike from the Sky: The Story of the Battle of Britain, McKee, Souvenir Press, £16.95.

Men of the Battle of Britain, Wynn, Gliddon Books, £25.00.

Reach for the Sky, Brickhin, New Portway, £10.95.

The Battle of Britain Aug-Oct, 1940, HMSO, £2.95.

The Few!, Collier/Kaplan, A&AP, £25.00.

The Hardest Day, Price, A&AP, £12.95.

Battle of Britain, Franks, Bison Books, £16.95.

Hurricane Squadron: No 87 Squadron at War, Adams, Air Research, £5.95.

The following titles have a Battle of Britain content, and also tell the reader about the aircraft and personalities that were involved.

Spitfire at War, Vol 1, Price, Ian Allan, £10.95.

Spitfire at War, Vol 2, Price, Ian Allan, £12.95.

Spitfire Special, Harron, Ian Allan, £5.95.

The Spitfire Story, Price, Cassell, £16.95.

The Hawker Hurricane, Mason, Aston, £18.95.

Combat Units of the Regia Aeronautica, (Italian AF 1940-43), Dunning, Air Research, £5.95.

British Aviation Colours of WW2, Arms & Armour Press, (Official Publication R/P), £10.95.

The Augsburg Eagle (BF109), Green, Aston, £15.95.

Eagles of the Third Reich, Mitcham, Airlife, £17.95.

Spitfire — The History, Morgan/Shacklady, Key, £39.95.

Ginger Lacy: Fighter Pilot, A&AP, £8.95.

Aircraft Archive, Fighters of World War Two, Vols 1 & 2, Argus Books, £5.95 (each).

All these books are available from the Royal Air Force Museum Shop, Dept AM, Hendon, London NW9 5LL. [Telephone 01-205 6867].

Mail Order

For UK, please add £2.50 to total order.
For overseas, please add £4.50 to total order.
Payment by cheque, PO, Visa, Mastercard, Eurocard, Access.
All overseas cheques, add £5.00 to cover bank charges.